The Purpose of Being Single: Embracing God's Plan and Walking in His Word

By Lillian Carlene Porter

To Oval Rikerson, My late sister(prayer partner) and Traci Wilkinson who encouraged me to write this book.

Other books by This Author:

The Purpose of Being Single Study Guide

The Purpose of Being Single
Embracing God's Plan and Walking in His Word

By Lillian Carlene Porter

Table of Contents

1. Embracing the Fullness of Singleness
2. State of a Single Woman
3. Instructions for a Single Woman
4. Purpose of the Single Woman is to Obey God
5. Praying for a Spouse
6. Epilogue
7. Meet the Author
8. Bibliography

INTRODUCTiON

Being single is often viewed as a waiting room—a season of anticipation, longing, or even frustration. But I believe there is a divine purpose in this period of our lives. It's not merely a placeholder for what's to come but an opportunity to discover who we are in God, to deepen our relationship with Him, and to grow in ways that are uniquely possible when we are single. While the world often defines singleness as a lack or something to be fixed, I see it as a special assignment from God, one that carries its own unique blessings, responsibilities, and callings.

From the beginning of my journey of singleness, God, in His infinite wisdom, guided me to the truth of His Word, which illuminated a different perspective. I realized that being single is not a waiting period; it is a divine appointment, a time for preparation, and an opportunity to fulfill a specific purpose that God has designed for us in this season.

Throughout this book, I will share my personal testimony—my triumphs, moments of clarity, and the revelations that have come from walking with God. I will also offer key advice rooted in the Word of God that has helped me navigate this journey. The Bible is filled with wisdom and instruction on how to live a fulfilling life, whether single or married. But as a single person, it is especially important to embrace the fullness of who God is calling us to be in this season. His Word offers guidance on how to walk with purpose, live with intention, and be content in the waiting, knowing that every moment is working together for our good and His glory.

Singleness is not a curse, nor is it a time to sit idly by, waiting for life to begin. It is a calling to be embraced and a unique season in which God's voice can be heard more clearly and His purpose more fully realized. My prayer is that through this book, you will gain a deeper understanding of what it means to be single in the eyes of God. May you find joy in the journey, strength in the scriptures, and clarity in

the call that God has placed on your life during this special season. Let us walk together, hand in hand with the Lord, discovering His perfect plan for our lives, whether we remain single or move into the next season He has prepared for us.

As we journey through this season of singleness, I want to provide you with seven steps on how to embrace being single in God's way while you wait on the possibility of a spouse—if that is His plan for your life. If marriage is not part of His purpose for you, these steps and accompanying scriptures will still guide you to live a fulfilling, joyful, and purposeful single life in alignment with God's will. Singleness is not a mere pause or a waiting room for something else to begin. It is a unique season filled with potential for growth, self-discovery, and a deeper relationship with God. My prayer is that this book will serve as a wonderful resource, guiding you to live a life that is pleasing to God and fulfilling in every sense.

Embracing the Fullness of Singleness

I was married for 21 years to a preacher, a Bishop, and for much of that time, I thought I understood what it meant to be a woman of God, to be a wife, and to follow the path laid out for me. I had grown up in a home that knew God, a home where prayer and worship were woven into the fabric of our daily lives. I had been taught to reverence God, to seek His will, and to stand firm in faith. So when I married, I expected that my life would be a testament to God's goodness, filled with joy, purpose, and partnership. But as the years went on, I began to see that some of the things I was going through in my marriage didn't align with God's Word or His promises. I could sense deep within my spirit that it wasn't all God. There were things that weren't right, and it wasn't just a matter of misunderstanding or miscommunication. I knew something was off.

I began to watch and pay closer attention to what was happening around me. I paid attention to the patterns, the behaviors, and the words that were spoken. I began to discern the difference between what was godly and what was simply tradition or control masked in the language of faith. And it was in that period of heightened awareness and discernment that God began to speak to me in ways that were undeniable. He started to pull back the layers and show me the truth of my situation. I remember the clarity of His voice as He told me to leave my husband. At first, I was shocked. How could this be? How could God tell me to leave a marriage, especially one to a preacher, a Bishop? This went against everything I had been taught about marriage and commitment. I struggled with the thought, questioned it, and prayed fervently for understanding. But God's direction was clear and consistent: it was time to leave.

Leaving wasn't easy. It took me ten years to finally divorce. Ten years of wrestling with God, myself, and the expectations of those around me. Ten years of questioning and seeking confirmation, of facing judgment and misunderstanding from people who couldn't see what God was showing me. But I knew deep down that God was leading me out of a situation that was not His will for me, and He was teaching me something in the process—about Himself, about His Word, and about what it truly means to walk in obedience.

During that time, God taught me the right way to read the Bible. Growing up in a Christian home and being married to a preacher, I thought I knew how to study the Word of God. I had read the Bible cover to cover, attended Bible studies, and listened to countless sermons. But in this season of my life, God was taking me deeper. He was showing me how to not just read the Bible but to read it with spiritual eyes, to understand it in the way He intended. It wasn't just about skimming over the surface or taking scriptures out of context; it was about diving deep into the truth and allowing the Holy Spirit to reveal His meaning to me.

Over a seven-year period, I made my way through the books of Moses. Seven years of slowly, deliberately, and carefully studying the Word, meditating on it day and night, and asking God to reveal His truth to me. There were moments of revelation that took my breath away and moments of confusion where I had to lean even harder into God for understanding. But through it all, I could feel myself growing stronger, more confident, and more in tune with God's voice.

Then, in 1994, God told me to read the book of Ezekiel. I remember opening the pages with anticipation, but as I started to read, I found myself struggling to understand. The visions, the symbolism, the prophetic language—it all felt overwhelming. I kept reading and praying, asking God to help me make sense of it. For a long time, I didn't understand it, but I kept going, trusting that God would give me clarity in His time.

And then it happened. I heard a lady speak on Ezekiel, and it was like a light bulb went off in my spirit. Suddenly, the pieces began to fit together, and I understood the message that God had been trying to convey to me all along. It wasn't just about understanding the words on the page; it was about understanding the heart of God, His character, His desires for His people, and His plans for redemption and restoration. I realized that God had been using those years of study to prepare me, to shape me, and to mold me into the woman He had called me to be.

That moment of clarity was life-changing. It was as if God had opened a door, and I could finally see the bigger picture. I saw how the experiences I had gone through in my marriage, the pain, the struggles, and the confusion were all part of a larger plan to draw me closer to Him and to teach me His ways. It was never about punishment or abandonment; it was about refining me, pruning me, and equipping me for the next chapter of my life.

Looking back now, I see how God was with me every step of the way, even when I felt lost and alone. He was teaching me how to listen to His voice, how to trust His timing, and how to walk in obedience even when it was difficult. Through His Word, He taught me how to be free—not just free from a marriage that was not His will, but free in Him, free to be who He created me to be, free to live out my purpose with boldness and confidence.

This journey has been anything but easy, but it has been worth it. And my hope is that by sharing my story, others will be encouraged to seek God for themselves, to listen to His voice, and to trust that He knows what is best. Whether you are in a difficult marriage, a challenging season, or simply seeking more of God, know that He is with you, guiding you, and speaking to you through His Word. All you have to do is be willing to listen, to trust, and to follow where He leads.

I remember a day that marked a turning point in my life, one I can't forget. I had been invited to a church by a prophetess who asked me to speak. To be honest, I didn't remember she had asked me to speak until I arrived and she mentioned it to me. In that moment, I was taken aback. I felt a rush of emotions. I hadn't prepared anything. I hadn't spent the time I normally would praying and seeking God about what to say, and now here I was, expected to deliver a message. But as I stood there, trying to gather my thoughts and my nerves, I was reminded that God always has a ram in the bush.

Though I hadn't prepared in the way I would have liked, God had been preparing me all along. Sometimes, we think we need to be ready in the ways that make sense to us, but God knows exactly what He's doing. In that moment, I decided to surrender to His leading, trusting that if He had allowed me to be in this position, He would also give me the words to speak. I felt a calm settle over me, and I began to speak from my heart about the power of a single woman, drawing on the experiences God had brought me through and the lessons He had taught me in my own journey.

I spoke about how being single is not a lesser state, nor is it a time to be pitied or to feel incomplete. Instead, it is a powerful, purposeful season that God can use to shape us, to grow us, and to set us apart for His divine purpose. I shared how I had learned to embrace my singleness, to see it as a gift rather than a burden, and how God had used this time in my life to bring me closer to Him and to reveal His calling over my life. As I spoke, I could feel the Spirit moving, guiding my words, and touching the hearts of those in the congregation.

After I finished speaking, the prophetess who had invited me came up to me with a look of amazement in her eyes. She told me that my message was meant to be in a book. She said that God had spoken to her and told her that this word needed to be shared far and wide, that it wasn't just for the people in that room, but for many others who needed to hear it. I stood there in awe, realizing that God had orchestrated this entire moment. She had no idea that I hadn't prepared, that I had forgotten I was even supposed to speak. She didn't know that I had been standing there, completely reliant on God to give me the words. Yet, she was confirming what I had felt deep in my spirit—that God wanted me to write about the purpose of being single.

That was the moment I knew I had to get started on this book. I knew God was calling me to share not just a single message but a comprehensive understanding of what it means to be single in His eyes. It was on June 23, 2019, that I first put pen to paper. I began writing, pouring out my heart and sharing the wisdom God had imparted to me over the years. I knew this book was not going to be just another self-help guide or a collection of thoughts. It was going to be a divinely inspired work, rooted in the Word of God, and led by the Spirit to empower, encourage, and uplift single women everywhere.

From the start, I felt God's hand on every word I wrote. I would sit down to write, and the words would flow, as if God Himself were guiding my pen. There were times when I would write for hours without stopping, so caught up in the inspiration that I lost all track of time. Other times, I would feel a block, a moment where I knew I needed to stop and pray, to seek God's guidance on what to say next. Every step of the way, I felt His presence, His leading, and His confirmation that this was the path He wanted me to take.

As I wrote, I often thought about 1 Corinthians 7:8-9, where Paul speaks about the benefits of being single and how it allows a person to focus on God without distraction. It became clear to me that God wants us to understand that singleness is not a lesser calling but a unique opportunity to serve Him with undivided devotion. It's a time to grow in our faith, to build a foundation that is unshakeable, and to discover the fullness of who we are in Christ. God has a purpose for each one of us, and being single is a significant part of that purpose for many.

Writing this book has been a journey of discovery for me as well. God has shown me so much about His love, His grace, and His plans for us as single people. He has reminded me that our value is not determined by our relationship status but by our relationship with Him. I've learned that being single is a time to be celebrated, a time to flourish, and a time to find joy in the unique ways God wants to use us.

As I continued to write, I realized that this book was not just for those who are currently single but also for those who have been single in the past, those who may find themselves single again in the future, and even for those who are married but want to better understand the single experience from a God-centered perspective. The principles of walking in obedience, trusting God's timing, and finding fulfillment in Him are universal, and they apply to every season of life.

My prayer is that this book will be a wonderful source of encouragement and a guide for those who want to live a life pleasing to God, regardless of their relationship status. I want every reader to walk away with a renewed sense of purpose, knowing that their singleness is not a curse but a calling. God has a plan for you, and whether that includes a spouse or not, His plans are always good, always perfect, and always designed to bring you closer to Him.

I encourage you to dive into this book with an open heart and a willingness to let God speak to you through His Word and through my experiences. I believe that as you read, you will find the answers you've been seeking, the encouragement you need, and the confirmation that God has a unique and wonderful plan for your life. Whether you are waiting for a spouse or embracing a life of singleness, know that God sees you, He loves you, and He has a purpose for you. May this book be a blessing to you as you walk out that purpose in faith, trust, and joy.

As I continued to write and reflect on the words of the Apostle Paul in 1 Corinthians 7:8-9, I realized the profound advice he was giving to single women. Paul, himself a single man, understood the unique challenges and opportunities that come with being unmarried. He spoke directly to those who were single, encouraging them to "abide" as he did. His message was clear: it is good to remain single, but if one cannot maintain self-control, it is better to marry than to burn with passion.

What does it mean to "abide," as Paul urged? To abide is to remain, to stay, to endure. In the context of singleness, it means to wait upon the Lord, to live in a way that is holy and pleasing to God, and to maintain a life of righteousness and purity. Abiding is not a passive act; it is an active choice to follow God's will, to serve Him wholeheartedly, and to remain faithful in the season He has placed us in. It means embracing where we are right now with a heart that seeks after God above all else.

For single women, this call to abide is not just a suggestion—it is a divine mandate. God is counting on us to stay holy, just as He is holy. In a world that often pressures us to compromise our values or to seek validation in relationships, the call to abide becomes even more significant. We are to stand firm in our faith, to live out our purpose with integrity, and to be lights in a world that desperately needs the love and truth of God.

When Paul advises that it is better to marry than to burn with passion, he acknowledges the very real human desires that God has given us. He recognizes that for some, singleness can be a difficult journey because of these desires. However, his point is not to rush into marriage out of fear or desperation but to recognize that marriage is a holy covenant, a sacred union that should not be entered into lightly. Marriage is beautiful and ordained by God, but it is not the ultimate goal; living a life that is pleasing to God is.

Being single is a unique opportunity to serve God without distraction, to pursue Him with all our heart, mind, and strength. It is a time when we can focus entirely on our relationship with God and on the assignments He has given us. This is not to say that married people cannot serve God wholeheartedly, but singleness offers a season where our devotion can be undivided.

So, how do we abide as single women in a way that is pleasing to God? We start by understanding that our identity is not defined by our relationship status but by our relationship with Christ. We are daughters of the King, beloved, and chosen, with a purpose that goes far beyond societal expectations. Abiding means waiting on God's timing, not rushing into relationships out of fear of being alone, but trusting that God's plans for us are good and perfect.

Abiding also means maintaining our purity, not just in the physical sense but in our thoughts, our actions, and our intentions. The world often tries to tell us that it is okay to compromise, to lower our standards, or to give in to temptation. But God calls us to a higher standard, to be holy as He is holy. This does not mean we are perfect, but it means we strive to live in a way that honors God, seeking His forgiveness when we fall short and relying on His strength to help us stand firm.

We abide by staying rooted in God's Word. The Bible is filled with wisdom and guidance for living a godly life. It is our source of strength, our comfort in times of loneliness, and our guide when we don't know which way to turn. When we meditate on God's Word and allow it to penetrate our hearts, we find the courage and the clarity we need to walk out our singleness with grace and confidence.

Prayer is another crucial aspect of abiding. It is our direct line of communication with God, where we can pour out our hearts, our desires, our frustrations, and our hopes. Prayer keeps us connected to the Father and reminds us that we are never truly alone. Through prayer, we gain insight into God's will for our lives, and we find the peace that surpasses all understanding, even in the midst of uncertainty.

Serving God is also a key component of abiding. As single women, we have a unique opportunity to dedicate our time, our talents, and our resources to God's kingdom. Whether it's volunteering at church, helping those in need, or simply being a light in our workplaces and communities, we can use this season to make a difference. God has given each of us gifts, and He wants us to use them to glorify Him and to bless others.

Finally, abiding means trusting God's plan for our lives. It means believing that He knows what is best for us, even when we don't understand. It means surrendering our will to His, knowing that His ways are higher than our ways and His thoughts higher than our thoughts. It means being content in every circumstance, knowing that our ultimate fulfillment comes not from a relationship with another person, but from a relationship with God.

If marriage is in God's plan for you, then trust that He will bring the right person into your life at the right time. But if marriage is not in His plan, know that you are still whole, still loved, and still called to a purpose that is just as significant. God sees you, He knows you, and He has a plan for you that is uniquely yours. As single women, we have the privilege of abiding in His presence, of growing in our faith, and of discovering the fullness of who we are in Him.

The journey of singleness is not always easy, but it is filled with opportunities for growth, for service, and for a deeper relationship with God. So, I encourage you to embrace this season, to abide in the Lord, and to trust that He is working all things together for your good. God is faithful, and He will never leave you nor forsake you. Stay strong, stay holy, and stay committed to the One who loves you most.

As single women abiding in the Lord, we are called to a deep and meaningful relationship with Him. Abiding is more than just waiting; it is about being anchored in God's Word and allowing it to shape and mold us into the women He has called us to be. It is a process of drilling into the depths of His Holy Word, seeking His face, and allowing His truth to perfect our walk with Him. Just as a craftsman refines a piece of art, God desires to refine our hearts, transforming us to love Him more fully and to live in a way that brings Him glory.

Abiding in God is an act of surrender, a conscious decision to place Him at the center of our lives and to trust His timing and His ways. It's about perfecting our hearts to see God, which means purifying our desires, our thoughts, and our actions so that they align with His will. This journey of abiding is one of continual growth, where our hearts are being improved to love Him as we love ourselves. When we love God with all our heart, soul, mind, and strength, we begin to understand His purpose for our lives, even in our singleness.

To abide as a single woman means to submit to God's will for your life, even if that includes remaining single for a time—or perhaps forever. It requires humility and a willingness to trust that God knows what is best for us. He sees the bigger picture, and His plans are always good. It's important to remember that if you cannot submit yourself to being a single woman in this season, your Heavenly Father understands. He knows your heart, your desires, and your struggles. He is compassionate, and He is with you every step of the way. But He also calls us to a higher standard, to seek His kingdom first, and to trust that everything else will be added to us according to His will.

Singleness is not a burden; it is a gift. It is a time for God to shape us, mold us, and prepare us for whatever lies ahead. But if you find that you cannot fully commit to being single, then you can rest in knowing that you have a Heavenly Father who is faithful, loving, and understanding. He knows your needs better than anyone else, and He is capable of meeting them in ways that far exceed your expectations.

As we reflect on the creation of Eve in Genesis 2:21-24, we see a beautiful picture of God's intention for relationships. The passage tells us, "So the Lord God caused the man to fall into a deep sleep; and while he was sleeping, he took one of the man's ribs and then closed up the place with flesh. Then the Lord God made a woman from the rib he had taken out of the man, and he brought her to the man. The man said, 'This is now bone of my bones and flesh of my flesh; she shall be called 'woman,' for she was taken out of man.' That is why a man leaves his father and mother and is united to his wife, and they become one flesh."

God created Eve as a companion for Adam, to complete him and to be a helper suitable for him. This was not an afterthought but a deliberate and purposeful act by God. Eve was created from Adam's rib, symbolizing that she was to stand by his side, not beneath him or above him. She was to be his partner, his equal, and together they were to fulfill God's purpose for their lives. This passage also highlights the sanctity and significance of marriage—a union where two become one flesh, a divine covenant established by God.

However, while marriage is a beautiful and sacred institution, it is not the ultimate goal for everyone. God's purpose for creating Eve was to fulfill His divine plan for humanity, and that plan looks different for each of us. For some, that means marriage, but for others, it may mean remaining single and serving God in other unique and impactful ways.

Single women, if you find yourself longing for a spouse, understand that this desire is natural and God-given. Yet, it is also important to recognize that your value and worth are not determined by your relationship status. God has a unique purpose for your life, and His plans are perfect. He may have a season of singleness for you to grow closer to Him, to serve Him without distraction, or to accomplish things that may not be possible within the confines of a marriage.

While the world often places pressure on us to be in a relationship, to marry, or to conform to societal expectations, God calls us to abide in Him first. He wants us to know Him deeply, to trust Him fully, and to serve Him wholeheartedly. When we abide in God, we position ourselves to hear His voice clearly and to understand His will for our lives.

For those who cannot fully embrace singleness, know that God sees your heart. He understands your desires and your struggles. If marriage is something He has placed in your heart, trust that He will provide the right person at the right time. But while you wait, use this time wisely. Grow in your relationship with God, develop your gifts and talents, serve others, and build a foundation that is rooted in Christ.

If you find that singleness is a challenge, remember that you are not alone. God is with you, and He is working in you to fulfill His purpose. He is using this season to prepare you for what is to come, whether that is marriage or a life of singleness dedicated to His service. Whatever the outcome, know that you are loved, valued, and chosen by God.

In abiding, we learn to be content in all circumstances, trusting that God's plans for us are far greater than anything we could imagine for ourselves. Whether you are called to be single for a season or for a lifetime, know that God has a purpose for you. Embrace it, live it, and trust that He is with you every step of the way.

To further expand on the profound themes presented in 1 Corinthians 7:32-35, let us delve deeper into the spiritual, emotional, and practical dimensions of singleness as an avenue for undistracted devotion to God. The goal is to explore the biblical, theological, and practical implications of this state of life, particularly for women, and to provide a comprehensive understanding of how singleness can be a season of incredible spiritual growth, service, and fulfillment.

1. The Biblical Foundation of Singleness

The Bible offers a rich tapestry of examples and teachings on singleness, reflecting the divine wisdom and diversity of life's circumstances. Paul, a single apostle himself, articulates his view on singleness not as a restriction but as a gift (1 Corinthians 7:7). In his letters, Paul emphasizes that both marriage and singleness are valuable in God's sight. Singleness, however, provides a unique platform for undivided devotion to the Lord.

Throughout Scripture, several prominent figures were single and used their lives to profoundly impact God's kingdom. Jesus Christ, the ultimate example of a holy life, was single, wholly dedicated to the Father's will. Other figures, such as John the Baptist, Anna the prophetess, Jeremiah, and possibly Mary Magdalene, showcase that God can use single individuals mightily for His purposes.

The Old Testament, while emphasizing family and lineage, still presents singleness as a powerful testimony of faith. Isaiah speaks of eunuchs who "hold fast to my covenant" and "choose what pleases me," promising them "a name better than sons and daughters" (Isaiah 56:4-5). This demonstrates that one's identity and worth in God's eyes are not determined by marital status but by faithfulness and obedience to Him.

2. Singleness as a Calling: Embracing the Gift

Many Christian women find themselves single by choice, circumstances, or divine calling. Each of these situations presents unique opportunities for spiritual growth and service. Viewing singleness as a calling rather than a limitation changes the narrative from waiting for the "next stage" to embracing the present with intentionality and purpose.

To embrace singleness as a gift is to understand that this season is appointed by God and has a divine purpose. This calling involves being set apart for the work of God, much like the Levites in the Old Testament who were dedicated solely to serve in the temple. Singleness is a sacred vocation that allows for full immersion in the things of God without the responsibilities or distractions that accompany marriage and family life.

Women who embrace singleness as a calling often find that they have more time and resources to devote to prayer, worship, service, and mission. It becomes a time to cultivate spiritual disciplines such as solitude, silence, and study, enabling a deeper relationship with God. This season is also a time to serve others more freely, whether through local church involvement, community service, global missions, or other ministries.

3. Deepening Intimacy with God

One of the most beautiful aspects of singleness is the opportunity to deepen one's intimacy with God. Without the emotional and physical demands of a spouse or children, a single woman can focus more fully on her relationship with Christ. This is a time to be "hidden in Christ" (Colossians 3:3), to find one's identity, worth, and security solely in Him.

Intimacy with God involves knowing Him personally and deeply. It means spending quality time in His presence, listening to His voice, and responding to His love. Developing this intimacy requires consistent spiritual disciplines—reading the Bible, meditating on Scripture, engaging in prayer, fasting, worship, and fellowship with other believers. It is through these practices that a single woman learns to recognize God's voice, discern His will, and experience His peace and joy.

Psalm 63:1 beautifully expresses this longing for intimacy with God: "O God, you are my God; earnestly I seek you; my soul thirsts for you; my flesh faints for you, as in a dry and weary land where there is no water." In singleness, the pursuit of God can become a singular focus. This deep communion with God shapes character, builds faith, and prepares a woman for whatever God has planned for her future.

4. Cultivating Holiness in Singleness

Holiness is a central theme in the Bible and a significant aspect of caring for the things that belong to the Lord. For a single woman, cultivating holiness means living a life set apart for God's purposes. It is about striving for purity in thought, word, and deed and reflecting the character of Christ in everyday life.

The pursuit of holiness involves a commitment to personal integrity and moral excellence. It requires vigilance in guarding one's heart and mind against influences that could lead to sin or compromise. Proverbs 4:23 reminds us, "Above all else, guard your heart, for everything you do flows from it." This guarding is an intentional effort to keep one's heart and mind focused on what is true, noble, right, pure, lovely, and admirable (Philippians 4:8).

In a world that often promotes self-gratification and instant pleasure, pursuing holiness requires countercultural choices. It means saying "no" to certain things that may be permissible but not beneficial (1 Corinthians 10:23). It involves setting boundaries in relationships, media consumption, and other areas of life to maintain spiritual and moral integrity. Holiness is not about legalism but about love—loving God so much that one desires to honor Him in every aspect of life.

5. Serving God's Kingdom: A Call to Action

A single woman's commitment to care for the things that belong to the Lord naturally extends to service. Jesus calls His followers to be the "salt of the earth" and the "light of the world" (Matthew 5:13-14). This calling is not limited to those who are married; it is a mandate for every believer. Single women, with their unique freedom and flexibility, can often serve in ways that those with family obligations cannot.

Service can take many forms. It may involve local ministry work such as teaching Sunday school, leading Bible studies, organizing community outreach, or serving in the church's worship team. It could also mean participating in or leading mission trips, advocating for social justice, volunteering at shelters, or mentoring younger women. The opportunities for service are endless, and God uses each person's unique gifts and passions to further His kingdom.

Moreover, service is not just about doing; it is also about being present. It is about being a source of encouragement, comfort, and strength to those around us. A single woman who cares for the things that belong to the Lord becomes a channel of His love and grace, ministering to others through her words, actions, and presence.

6. Finding Fulfillment and Contentment

One of the challenges that single women may face is the pressure to view marriage as the ultimate goal or a source of fulfillment. However, true fulfillment comes from knowing and doing God's will. It comes from living a life that is fully surrendered to Christ, whether single or married. Contentment is a spiritual discipline that involves trusting God's timing and provision, being grateful for His blessings, and finding joy in His presence.

Philippians 4:11-13 speaks to this contentment: "I have learned in whatever situation I am to be content. I know how to be brought low, and I know how to abound. In any and every circumstance, I have learned the secret of facing plenty and hunger, abundance and need. I can do all things through him who strengthens me." Contentment is about trusting that God's plans are good and that He is enough, regardless of one's circumstances.

Singleness can be a season of abundant joy, peace, and purpose when one chooses to focus on God rather than what is lacking. It is a time to cultivate gratitude, to celebrate God's faithfulness, and to enjoy the freedom to serve and grow in ways that may not be possible in other seasons of life.

7. Building a Legacy of Faith

For single women who care for the things that belong to the Lord, there is also the opportunity to build a lasting legacy of faith. This legacy is not about fame or recognition; it is about leaving an imprint on the lives of others through love, service, and discipleship. It is about investing in the next generation, raising up spiritual sons and daughters, and impacting the world for Christ.

A legacy of faith is built through intentional relationships, mentorship, and discipleship. It involves pouring into others what God has poured into you—sharing wisdom, experiences, and spiritual insights that can help others grow in their walk with God. It means being a spiritual mother, sister, or friend to those who need encouragement, guidance, and support.

8. Navigating Challenges and Finding Strength in Community

Singleness, like any season of life, comes with its own set of challenges. Loneliness, societal pressure, and unmet desires are real struggles that single women may face. However, these challenges can be opportunities for growth, dependence on God, and deeper community with others.

Navigating these challenges requires a support system—a community of believers who can provide encouragement, accountability, and companionship. The local church is meant to be a family where single women are valued, supported, and included. Being part of a small group, Bible study, or ministry team can provide the relational support needed to thrive in singleness.

Furthermore, mentorship can be invaluable. Older women who have walked the path of singleness or have wisdom from their own journeys can offer guidance and encouragement. Titus 2:3-5 speaks to the importance of older women teaching and encouraging younger women. This intergenerational mentorship is a beautiful picture of the body of Christ working together to build each other up.

13. Addressing Loneliness and Social Pressures

Loneliness and societal pressures can be significant challenges for single women. Understanding and addressing these challenges is essential for maintaining a healthy and joyful life in singleness.

1. Combatting Loneliness: Loneliness is a common experience in singleness, but it can be addressed through intentional community and meaningful relationships. Reach out to friends, family, and fellow believers. Join groups and activities that align with your interests and values. Building connections and nurturing relationships can help alleviate feelings of isolation.

2. Managing Societal Pressures: Society often places a high value on marriage and family, which can lead to feelings of inadequacy or pressure for those who are single. It's important to remember that your worth and value are not determined by marital status. Focus on your identity in Christ and the unique contributions you can make to God's kingdom.

3. Finding Fulfillment in Purpose: Embrace your current season with a sense of purpose and fulfillment. Engage in activities and pursuits that bring joy and satisfaction. Recognize that your life has meaning and impact, regardless of your marital status.

4. Navigating Cultural Expectations: Be aware of cultural expectations and norms that may influence your perception of singleness. Challenge stereotypes and misconceptions about single life. Embrace a perspective that aligns with biblical teachings and your personal experience.

14. Preparing for Potential Future Transitions

While embracing the present season of singleness, it's also valuable to prepare for potential future transitions, whether that involves marriage, a different calling, or another significant life change. Preparation involves both practical and spiritual readiness.

1. Building Strong Foundations: Invest in developing strong spiritual, emotional, and relational foundations. Building resilience, wisdom, and emotional intelligence will serve you well in any future transition.

2. Seeking God's Guidance: Continually seek God's guidance and direction for your life. Remain open to His leading and be prepared to respond to His call, whatever it may be. Prayerfully consider any changes or opportunities that come your way.

3. Preparing for Marriage: If marriage is a future possibility, use this time to prepare for a healthy and Christ-centered relationship. Consider premarital counseling, study relationship dynamics, and cultivate qualities that will contribute to a strong and loving marriage.

4. Embracing Change: Life transitions often bring change and uncertainty. Embrace change with faith and trust in God's plan. Prepare yourself mentally and spiritually to adapt to new roles and responsibilities.

15. Celebrating the Journey of Singleness

Celebrating the journey of singleness involves recognizing and appreciating the unique opportunities and experiences that this season provides. It is a time to celebrate God's goodness, reflect on personal growth, and embrace the joy that comes from living out one's faith.

1. Acknowledging Achievements: Take time to acknowledge and celebrate your achievements and milestones during this season. Reflect on the growth, accomplishments, and positive impacts you have made.
2. Expressing Gratitude: Cultivate a spirit of gratitude for the blessings and opportunities that singleness brings. Thank God for the freedom, experiences, and growth that come with this season.
3. Sharing Your Story: Share your journey and experiences with others. Your story can inspire and encourage others who are navigating similar paths. Be open about the challenges and triumphs, and offer support and wisdom to those who may benefit from your insights.
4. Embracing Joy: Find joy in the present moment and celebrate the life you are living. Enjoy the freedom, flexibility, and opportunities that singleness provides. Embrace the journey with a heart full of joy and gratitude.

1 Corinthians 7:32-35 offers a powerful perspective on singleness, highlighting its potential for undivided devotion to God. Singleness is not a lesser state but a unique and honorable calling with its own set of opportunities and blessings. It is a season that allows for deep spiritual growth, focused service, and intimate relationship with God.

As single women embrace this season, they can experience the richness of God's grace, the joy of living out their faith, and the fulfillment of serving His kingdom. Singleness is a time to grow, to serve, and to celebrate the journey with gratitude and purpose. Whether single or married, the ultimate goal is to know God, to love Him, and to serve Him with all that we are.

May each woman who navigates this season of singleness find peace, purpose, and fulfillment as she walks this path with God by her side. Embrace the journey with faith, joy, and a deep sense of divine calling, knowing that God's plans are good and His love is unwavering.

State of a Single Woman

In Acts 2:46-47, we see a vivid depiction of the early church's communal life. They gathered daily in the temple courts and broke bread together in their homes, sharing meals with glad and sincere hearts. This passage highlights the importance of hospitality as a cornerstone of the early Christian community. Their practice of breaking bread and enjoying each other's company wasn't just about eating; it was about building a deep sense of fellowship and mutual support that fueled the growth of the church.

As a single woman, I find that hospitality offers me a unique and powerful way to live out my faith and contribute to the community. Without the immediate responsibilities of a spouse or children, I have the flexibility to open my home, prepare meals, and care for others in a way that might be more challenging for those who are married. I can dedicate time and energy to hosting gatherings, which allows me to respond to needs and opportunities for service as they arise.

For me, practicing hospitality is about more than just providing food. It's about creating a space where people feel welcomed, valued, and connected. Since 2013, I have taken it upon myself to feed people, often following a sense of calling from the Lord. Preparing meals and distributing them to those in need isn't just a task; it's a way to show love, support, and to live out the command to "share with the Lord's people who are in need" (Romans 12:13). This act of service is deeply rooted in the biblical principle of hospitality, which is emphasized throughout Scripture.

In my experience, hospitality has proven to be a meaningful expression of faith. For instance, inviting people into my home for meals and fellowship mirrors the early church's practice as described in Acts. It allows me to foster a sense of community and contribute to spiritual growth, not just for myself, but for others as well. Each meal and gathering becomes an opportunity to build relationships and strengthen the bonds within the community.

However, practicing hospitality does come with its challenges. Financial constraints or a busy schedule can sometimes limit what I'm able to offer. Yet, I've learned that hospitality doesn't require extravagance; it's about thoughtfulness and care. Additionally, I've had to navigate feelings of loneliness or isolation, which can make it challenging to focus on serving others. Finding a supportive network and connecting with like-minded individuals has been crucial in overcoming these obstacles.

Despite these challenges, the spiritual impact of hospitality is profound. It enhances my spiritual growth, strengthens my faith, and fosters a supportive community. Each act of hospitality serves as a reminder of God's love and grace and contributes to building a vibrant church community.

Looking at biblical examples like Abraham and Sarah, Lydia, and Martha, I see models of hospitality that inspire and encourage me. Their acts of welcoming and serving others are a testament to the value of this practice in the life of a believer. Their stories remind me of the significance of hospitality and motivate me to embrace this role wholeheartedly.

As I continue to practice hospitality, I find fulfillment and purpose in serving others and contributing to the church community. It is a significant way to embody the love of Christ and to make a meaningful impact. I embrace this calling with gratitude, knowing that my efforts are valued and that they play a vital role in building a caring and supportive community. Through hospitality, I am able to live out my faith in a tangible and impactful way, and for that, I am deeply grateful.

Being a single woman encompasses both practical and spiritual dimensions. Often, singleness is perceived as a phase or temporary condition, but from a Christian perspective, it can hold profound significance and contribute meaningfully to the Kingdom of God. This exploration delves into how being single can be understood as an opportunity for growth, service, and devotion, aligned with God's promises and purpose.

To begin, it's crucial to understand the meaning of "state." In general, the term can be understood in several contexts:

- **Condition**: The condition or situation in which someone finds themselves at a particular time, including physical, emotional, and spiritual states.

- **Status**: The position or status of an individual, such as being single, married, or a student.

- **State of Mind**: The mental or emotional attitude a person maintains, which affects their actions and outlook.

- **State of Being**: A holistic term encompassing an individual's entire set of circumstances and well-being.

- **Temporal State**: A temporary or transient condition, emphasizing that certain states are not permanent but subject to change.

In this context, "state" refers to both the condition of being single and the broader state of mind and spiritual condition that comes with it.

Being a single woman offers unique opportunities to serve and contribute to the Kingdom of God. Singleness can be a time of profound growth and impact, offering possibilities different from those in married life. For instance, single women often have more time and flexibility compared to those with family responsibilities. This availability can be directed toward ministry, service, and personal growth. Without the immediate demands of a spouse or children, single women can dedicate their time to various forms of service, such as volunteer work, church activities, and outreach programs.

The Apostle Paul highlights the advantages of singleness in 1 Corinthians 7:32-35, noting that a single person can focus on serving the Lord without the divided interests that come with marital responsibilities. This undivided devotion allows single women to pursue spiritual growth, study, and prayer with greater intensity. Moreover, hospitality is a significant aspect of Christian life. Single women can use their homes and resources to host gatherings, provide meals, and offer support to others. This practice not only builds community but also reflects God's love and generosity.

Additionally, the way a single woman lives her life can serve as a powerful testimony to others. Her commitment to faith, handling of challenges, and active involvement in church life can inspire and encourage those around her. Singleness also provides an opportunity for personal development and preparation for future roles, whether in ministry, career, or personal life. It allows for the cultivation of skills, deepening of faith, and preparation for potential future responsibilities.

God's promises are often associated with fulfillment and completeness and extend to every state of life, including singleness. Understanding and embracing these promises can transform one's perspective on their current state and contribute to their role in the Kingdom of God. For instance, God promises to be with us always (Matthew 28:20). Regardless of our state, whether single or married, we can rely on His constant presence and support. This assurance provides comfort and strength as we navigate our circumstances.

Philippians 4:19 assures us that God will supply all our needs according to His riches in glory. This promise holds true in every state, and single women can trust in God's provision for their physical, emotional, and spiritual needs. God has a purpose for each person, as seen in Jeremiah 29:11. Even in singleness, there is a divine plan and purpose that can be fulfilled through faithful living and service. Embracing this promise helps single women understand their role and contribution to God's Kingdom.

John 15:11 speaks of the joy that comes from abiding in Christ. This joy is not dependent on marital status but on a relationship with God. Single women can experience and share this joy, impacting others and enhancing their own spiritual journey. Romans 8:28 assures that God works all things for the good of those who love Him. This promise extends to every state of life, including singleness. God uses every circumstance to shape and transform us into the image of Christ.

The state of mind plays a crucial role in how we experience and handle our circumstances. For single women, maintaining a state of mind focused on God can lead to spiritual growth and fulfillment. Philippians 4:11-13 teaches contentment in every situation. Cultivating a mindset of contentment allows single women to find peace and joy in their current state rather than yearning for a different situation.

Embracing a mindset of service and generosity enables single women to use their unique opportunities to impact others. Serving others can bring a sense of purpose and fulfillment, aligning with God's call to love and care for our neighbors. Trusting in God's plan and timing is essential. Proverbs 3:5-6 encourages us to trust in the Lord and lean not on our understanding. This trust allows single women to navigate their circumstances with confidence and hope.

Joy, as a fruit of the Spirit (Galatians 5:22-23), can be experienced regardless of marital status. Cultivating a joyful attitude helps single women reflect God's love and grace to others. Viewing singleness as an opportunity for personal and spiritual growth can be empowering. Investing time in prayer, study, and self-improvement can lead to deeper spiritual insights and a stronger relationship with God.

Several biblical figures demonstrate how singleness can contribute to God's Kingdom. For example, Paul's singleness allowed him to travel extensively, plant churches, and write letters that form a significant part of the New Testament. His life is a testament to the impact that can be made through dedicated service and focus. Jesus, as the ultimate example, lived a single life devoted to His mission of salvation. His life and ministry exemplify the profound impact that can be made through a focused and sacrificial life. Anna the Prophetess, in Luke 2:36-38, dedicated herself to fasting and prayer in the temple. Her devotion and prophetic witness were instrumental in recognizing Jesus as the Messiah.

For single women navigating their role in the Kingdom of God, encouragement is vital. Recognize and appreciate the unique contributions you make as a single woman. Your role in the church and community is significant and valued. Seek community and support by connecting with others who share your passion for service and growth. Building a supportive network can provide encouragement and opportunities for collaboration. Embrace the opportunities that come your way, whether in ministry, career, or personal development. God often uses our unique circumstances to fulfill His purposes. Trust in God's plan and timing, and remain hopeful. Your current state is part of a larger divine plan, and God's promises will guide and sustain you.

The state of being a single woman is not merely a transitional phase but a significant and purposeful position within the Kingdom of God. Embracing this state with a focus on God's promises and maintaining a positive state of mind can lead to profound spiritual growth and impactful service. By understanding and living out the role of singleness, single women can make meaningful contributions to the church and the broader community, reflecting the love and grace of Christ in their lives. In this journey, may single women find fulfillment, purpose, and joy, knowing that their contributions are valued and their lives are a testament to God's love and faithfulness.

The state of being single often feels like a transitional phase, but from a Christian perspective, it holds significant spiritual and practical opportunities. Embracing singleness can offer a unique alignment with God and the Holy Spirit, providing a space for profound growth and service.

Understanding the concept of "state" in this context is crucial. In general terms, a state can refer to our condition, status, state of mind, or even a temporary situation. For me, being single is not just a status but a holistic state encompassing physical, emotional, and spiritual aspects. This period of my life presents a unique opportunity to align fully with God's will and deepen my relationship with Him.

1 Corinthians 6:19-20 reminds me that my body is a temple of the Holy Spirit. This passage emphasizes that I am not my own but have been bought at a price, urging me to honor God with my body. As a single person, this understanding is particularly impactful. I have the chance to focus on living a life that respects and honors God, utilizing my time to cultivate spiritual disciplines and maintain purity. My physical and spiritual health become intertwined in a way that allows me to fully embrace the presence of the Holy Spirit within me.

Singleness offers a unique opportunity to develop a deeper relationship with the Holy Spirit. Without the immediate responsibilities that come with marriage, I have more time for prayer, meditation, and spiritual growth. This alignment fosters a stronger connection with God, enabling me to discern His will more clearly and live out His purpose with greater focus.

Philippians 4:13 speaks to me about the empowerment I receive through my relationship with Christ. The verse assures me that I can do all things through Christ who strengthens me. This empowerment is particularly relevant during this period of singleness. With fewer immediate responsibilities, I can dedicate my energy to spiritual and personal development, overcoming challenges and seizing opportunities for service. Christ's strength enables me to navigate feelings of loneliness or societal pressures, allowing me to pursue spiritual goals and achieve milestones that align with God's will.

Romans 12:1 calls me to present myself as a living sacrifice, holy and pleasing to God. This call to dedicate every aspect of my life to Him is especially poignant in singleness. Without the distractions of marital life, I can focus on offering my time, talents, and resources fully to God's work. This dedication involves aligning my actions, thoughts, and desires with His will, allowing Him to use me for His purposes and leading to personal transformation.

Living as a living sacrifice means embracing both practical and spiritual aspects of dedication. I can use my time to serve others, engage in ministry, and participate in acts of kindness, reflecting God's love and grace. This lifestyle leads to personal growth, shaping my character and guiding my actions in alignment with His will.

John 6:35 reminds me that true fulfillment is found in Christ alone. Jesus' promise that He is the bread of life assures me that my deepest needs and desires are met in Him. Singleness can bring feelings of loneliness, but this promise helps me find satisfaction in my relationship with Christ. By anchoring my identity and fulfillment in Him, I can navigate my state of singleness with peace and contentment, breaking free from any discontent that may arise.

When I find my fulfillment in Christ, it transforms how I live and interact with others. I approach life with a sense of purpose and joy, reflecting the satisfaction and contentment that come from a relationship with Him. This fulfillment enables me to serve others, engage in meaningful activities, and live out my faith with greater impact.

In embracing singleness with a heart dedicated to God, I discover profound opportunities for growth, service, and fulfillment. By aligning with God's promises and understanding the unique potential of this state, I can make a meaningful impact on the Kingdom of God and reflect His love and grace to the world. May this journey through singleness lead me to deeper joy, purpose, and fulfillment, knowing that my life is a testament to His love and faithfulness.

Being single is often viewed through a lens of transition or as a mere phase before moving on to another life stage. However, I've come to realize that my singlehood is not just a temporary condition but a profound opportunity to align deeply with God and embrace my spiritual journey. Understanding the state of being single encompasses both practical and spiritual dimensions, and it is essential to recognize the significant impact this period can have on my relationship with God and my role in His Kingdom.

Firstly, to fully grasp the essence of my state as a single woman, it is important to understand what "state" means in various contexts. In everyday life, "state" can refer to my condition—physical, emotional, or spiritual. It can also denote my status, such as being single, and how I interact with my circumstances. Additionally, "state of mind" reflects my mental and emotional attitude, while "state of being" encompasses the entirety of my experience and well-being. For me, singleness is not merely a status but a holistic state that integrates my physical, emotional, and spiritual condition.

Reflecting on 1 Corinthians 6:19-20, I recognize that my body is a temple of the Holy Spirit. This passage profoundly influences how I approach my single life. The understanding that I am not my own but have been bought at a price encourages me to honor God with my body. This period of singleness provides a unique opportunity to dedicate myself entirely to spiritual growth, living a life of purity and devotion. The absence of marital responsibilities allows me to focus more on nurturing my relationship with God and engaging deeply with the Holy Spirit. This focus fosters a strong alignment with God's will and His purpose for my life, making my singlehood a time of profound spiritual enrichment.

Philippians 4:13 reassures me of the strength I have through Christ. The verse, "I can do all things through Christ who strengthens me," is especially relevant during this time. Singleness can present its own set of challenges, including societal expectations and personal struggles with loneliness. Yet, knowing that Christ empowers me through every situation allows me to navigate these challenges with confidence. This empowerment extends to my ability to pursue spiritual and personal goals, serve others, and overcome obstacles. Christ's strength provides me with the resilience and courage needed to make the most of this period in my life.

Romans 12:1 calls me to present myself as a living sacrifice, holy and pleasing to God. This call to dedicate every aspect of my life to Him becomes particularly meaningful in singleness. With fewer distractions from marital responsibilities, I have the space to focus on offering my time, talents, and resources fully to God's work. This dedication involves aligning my actions, thoughts, and desires with His will. By living as a living sacrifice, I commit myself to serve others, engage in ministry, and participate in acts of kindness, reflecting God's love and grace. This lifestyle leads to personal transformation, shaping my character and guiding my actions in alignment with His purpose.

In embracing my role as a living sacrifice, I find myself immersed in both practical and spiritual acts of dedication. The ability to serve others and engage in meaningful activities becomes a central aspect of my life. This period of singleness allows me to invest my time and energy into initiatives that align with God's will, whether through volunteering, participating in church activities, or supporting outreach programs. Such engagements not only benefit others but also enrich my spiritual journey, leading to deeper fulfillment and purpose.

John 6:35, where Jesus declares, "I am the bread of life," speaks directly to the core of my experience in singleness. This promise assures me that true fulfillment comes from Christ alone. While singleness can sometimes bring about feelings of loneliness or societal pressure, this verse reminds me that my deepest needs and desires are met in Him. Finding satisfaction in my relationship with Christ transforms how I navigate my single life. It enables me to approach each day with a sense of peace and contentment, rather than yearning for a different situation.

This fulfillment in Christ affects my interactions with others and my approach to life. When I find my contentment in Him, I am better equipped to reflect His love and grace to those around me. My sense of purpose becomes clearer, and my actions are more aligned with His will. The joy and satisfaction that come from a relationship with Christ empower me to serve others, engage in meaningful endeavors, and live out my faith with greater impact.

In embracing the state of singleness with a heart fully devoted to God, I discover profound opportunities for growth, service, and fulfillment. By aligning with His promises and understanding the unique potential of this phase of life, I can make significant contributions to His Kingdom and reflect His love and grace to the world. This journey through singleness is not just about waiting for the next phase but about living fully in the present, recognizing that my life, in this state, is a testament to God's love, faithfulness, and purpose.

As I navigate the journey of being a single woman, the profound truth found in John 6:35 resonates deeply within me. When Jesus says, "I am the bread of life: he that comes to me shall never hunger; and he that believes on me shall never thirst," it redefines my perspective on fulfillment and contentment. This promise of complete satisfaction in Christ is a guiding principle for me, shaping how I approach my life, relationships, and daily experiences. Embracing this truth means recognizing that my deepest needs and longings are met not through external circumstances or future expectations but through a relationship with Jesus Christ. This understanding becomes a cornerstone of my spiritual journey and helps me maintain a sense of peace and fulfillment in my singlehood.

In my daily life, I continually seek to embody the essence of this verse. I remind myself that no matter what my current state might be, true contentment comes from within, rooted in my relationship with Christ. The societal pressures and personal challenges of being single can sometimes lead to feelings of inadequacy or desire for more. Yet, the promise that Jesus is the bread of life assures me that my worth and satisfaction are not dependent on my marital status or any other external factor. By focusing on Him and trusting in His provision, I find that my hunger and thirst for significance and belonging are wholly addressed by His presence in my life.

Hebrews 13:5 also provides valuable insight into how I should conduct myself as a single woman. The scripture states, "Let your conversation be without covetousness; and be content with such things as ye have." This call to contentment and integrity in speech is especially relevant in my life. As a single woman, I am aware that my conversations and interactions can greatly influence how I perceive my own situation and how others perceive me. It is crucial for me to guard against covetousness and discontentment in my dialogue, whether with friends, family, or in my own thoughts.

My conversations reflect my inner state of mind and heart. If I am focused on what I lack or what I desire, it can lead to a sense of dissatisfaction and can affect my interactions with others. Therefore, I strive to ensure that my conversations are marked by gratitude and positivity. By aligning my speech with a sense of contentment, I not only uplift myself but also contribute to a more positive and supportive environment for those around me. This practice helps me maintain a healthy perspective on my singlehood, seeing it as a valuable period of growth and service rather than a mere waiting room for a different stage of life.

Moreover, being mindful of my conversations involves being honest about my feelings while also being careful not to let them overshadow the blessings I currently enjoy. I am learning to express my thoughts and experiences in ways that reflect my trust in God's plan and my appreciation for the journey He has placed me on. This approach transforms how I engage with others and how I perceive my own situation, leading to a more fulfilling and joyful experience of singleness.

In embracing my singlehood with a focus on Christ's promise and a commitment to contentment, I find that my life takes on a new depth of meaning. My relationship with Jesus becomes the center of my existence, providing me with a sense of purpose and direction. As I continue to walk this path, I am reminded that my value and fulfillment come from Him alone, and not from the changes or additions that might come in the future.

Furthermore, maintaining a conversation without covetousness also means resisting the temptation to compare my life with others. It is easy to look at friends or acquaintances who are married and feel a sense of envy or inadequacy. However, by keeping my focus on Jesus and being content with my current state, I can avoid these pitfalls. I choose to celebrate the unique opportunities and experiences that come with being single, rather than dwelling on what I might perceive as lacking.

In practical terms, this means actively engaging in activities and pursuits that align with my values and passions. It means using my time and resources to contribute to my community, support others, and grow in my faith. By investing in these areas, I find that my life becomes richer and more fulfilling, reflecting the joy and contentment that comes from a relationship with Christ.

Additionally, the journey of singlehood is not just about personal growth but also about how I impact those around me. My attitudes and actions can serve as a testimony to the strength and peace that comes from trusting in God. By living out the principles of John 6:35 and Hebrews 13:5, I have the opportunity to be a source of encouragement and inspiration to others who may be navigating similar experiences. My life can demonstrate that true fulfillment and satisfaction are found in Christ, regardless of one's circumstances.

In conclusion, embracing the state of being single involves a deep understanding of spiritual truths and a commitment to living them out in everyday life. By focusing on Christ as the bread of life and maintaining a conversation marked by contentment, I am able to find profound fulfillment and joy in my current situation. This approach not only enriches my own experience but also serves as a testament to the transformative power of a relationship with Jesus. As I continue on this journey, I am grateful for the opportunities it provides for growth, service, and deeper connection with God, trusting that He is guiding me through every step of the way.

In my journey as a single woman, I find profound encouragement and purpose in the words of Acts 2:47, which say, "Praising God and having favor with all the people. And the Lord added to the church daily those who were being saved." This verse not only highlights the importance of praise and favor in our daily lives but also illustrates how our personal and communal faith can contribute to the expansion of God's Kingdom. It is a reminder that, as single women, we have a significant role to play in spreading the Word of God and adding to the Church. By living out our faith authentically and embracing our unique position, we can make meaningful contributions to the Kingdom of God.

For me, the act of praising God is central to how I approach each day. It is not merely a ritual but a way of life that reflects my gratitude and commitment to the Lord. In my daily routines, I strive to incorporate praise into every aspect of my life, from the mundane to the extraordinary. This practice of worship is a powerful expression of my relationship with God and serves as a testament to His goodness and grace. By praising God in my thoughts, words, and actions, I align myself with His will and invite His presence into my life, which helps me navigate the challenges and joys of singlehood with a heart full of gratitude.

Having favor with all people, as described in Acts 2:47, is another important aspect of my journey. It involves cultivating positive relationships and being a source of encouragement and support to those around me. I recognize that my interactions with others can either reflect the love of Christ or detract from it. Therefore, I strive to approach each relationship with kindness, understanding, and a genuine desire to uplift others. By doing so, I create an environment where God's love is evident, and where people feel valued and appreciated. This approach not only enhances my personal relationships but also contributes to a broader sense of community and fellowship that reflects God's Kingdom.

The verse also speaks to the growth of the Church through the daily addition of new believers. This growth is a direct result of the faithful witness and outreach of the early Christians, who lived out their faith in a way that attracted others to Christ. As a single woman, I am inspired by this example and seek to emulate it in my own life. I recognize that my daily actions, words, and choices can influence others and potentially lead them to a deeper understanding of God's love and salvation. Whether through casual conversations, acts of service, or simply living out my faith with authenticity, I strive to be a vessel through which others can experience the grace and truth of Jesus Christ.

In my commitment to adding to the Kingdom of God, I also focus on how God reigns as King in my life. This means acknowledging His sovereignty in every aspect of my existence and allowing Him to guide my decisions, actions, and relationships. It involves submitting to His will and trusting in His plan for my life, even when I may not fully understand it. By prioritizing God's Kingdom and seeking His guidance, I am able to align my life with His purposes and contribute to the growth of His Church.

Being single provides a unique opportunity to dedicate more time and energy to the work of God's Kingdom. Without the responsibilities of a spouse or children, I have the flexibility to engage in various forms of ministry and service. This might include volunteering, participating in church activities, or supporting outreach efforts. Each of these opportunities allows me to contribute to the spread of the Gospel and the expansion of God's Kingdom in tangible ways. By embracing these opportunities with a willing heart, I am able to make a positive impact and fulfill my role in God's grand plan.

In addition to practical involvement, I also focus on cultivating a personal relationship with God that is deeply rooted in prayer and study. This relationship is the foundation of my ability to contribute effectively to the Kingdom of God. Through prayer, I seek God's guidance, strength, and wisdom, asking Him to help me navigate the challenges of singlehood and to use my life for His glory. Through studying the Scriptures, I gain a deeper understanding of His will and His promises, which informs how I live and serve.

I am also mindful of the power of my testimony. By living a life that reflects God's love and grace, I have the opportunity to share my faith story with others. My experiences, challenges, and triumphs can serve as a testimony to the power of God in my life, potentially inspiring others to seek a relationship with Him. This aspect of my journey is deeply fulfilling, as it allows me to be a witness to the transformative power of God's love and to contribute to the growth of His Kingdom.

My role as a single woman in expanding the Kingdom of God is both significant and rewarding. By praising God, cultivating positive relationships, and living out my faith with authenticity, I contribute to the growth of the Church and the spread of the Gospel. Embracing God's sovereignty in my life and dedicating myself to His work allows me to make meaningful contributions to His Kingdom. As I continue on this journey, I am committed to reflecting God's love, seeking His guidance, and using my life to advance His purposes. Through these efforts, I find fulfillment and purpose, knowing that my life is a testament to His grace and a contribution to the expansion of His Kingdom.

As a single woman, I deeply recognize the unique opportunities and responsibilities that accompany this phase of life. This season offers a profound chance for growth and fulfillment, as I am acutely aware of the promise that God has a plan for each of us, including our journey toward marriage, if that aligns with His divine will. The comforting assurance that "Singles, get on board, God will bring that husband in due time" serves as a powerful reminder that God's timing is always perfect, even when His plan may not be immediately apparent to us. Just as Jesus came to redeem humanity, and His reign as King is central to our faith, we too, as single women, operate within His kingship to fulfill a divine purpose.

Jesus's mission on earth was clear and transformative. He came to redeem humanity, a central aspect of His purpose that reshaped the course of history. In much the same way, our mission as single women involves operating within the framework of His kingship with dedication and faithfulness. Our roles, while distinct from Jesus's redemptive work, are equally significant. We are called to share the Word of God, embody His promises, and impact those around us in profound ways. This call to actively participate in the Kingdom work requires us to be vessels through which God's love and truth are communicated, thereby contributing to the unfolding of His divine plans.

Being single uniquely positions us to embrace this role within the Kingdom. Without the immediate responsibilities of a spouse or children, we often have greater flexibility to engage deeply in ministry, personal growth, and service. This period of singleness can be viewed as a time of preparation and opportunity, allowing us to devote ourselves more fully to the work of the Kingdom. By focusing on spiritual growth, serving others, and living out God's promises, we become active participants in the greater mission of redemption and transformation that Jesus initiated.

One of the most profound aspects of this role is the capacity to contribute to the redemption of others through the power of God's Word. Redemption extends beyond personal salvation; it involves bringing others into the light of Christ. As we live out our faith, share the Gospel, and support those around us, we participate in the ongoing work of redemption that Jesus began. This call to be active in our faith invites us to engage with others meaningfully and to use our gifts and opportunities to advance the Kingdom of God.

The promise of God's governance, as expressed in Scripture, is a pivotal element of our mission. God's governance encompasses His rule, His guidance, and His ultimate plan for humanity. By aligning ourselves with His will and living out His promises, we become part of His governance, reflecting His values and purpose in our lives. This alignment requires a commitment to seeking His guidance, adhering to His commands, and trusting His plan for our lives.

Operating within the kingship of Jesus also means that we are called to pray for His will to be done on earth as it is in heaven. This prayer, commonly known as the Lord's Prayer, is a powerful declaration of our desire for God's Kingdom to be established and His purposes to be fulfilled. By praying this prayer and striving to live in accordance with it, we contribute to the manifestation of God's will on earth. Our actions, words, and decisions should reflect this desire, as we work to bring about His Kingdom through our daily lives.

In practical terms, this focus on living out the values of the Kingdom, such as love, justice, and compassion, is crucial. By embodying these values, we demonstrate the reality of God's Kingdom and invite others to experience His presence and grace. This call to live with intention and purpose means recognizing that our actions and attitudes have the potential to impact others and contribute to the growth of the Kingdom.

Additionally, this period of singleness offers a unique opportunity to deepen our relationship with God. It is a time to build a strong spiritual foundation, engage in personal prayer and study, and develop a deeper understanding of His Word. By investing in our spiritual growth, we prepare ourselves to fulfill the role that God has for us, whether that includes future marriage, continued singleness, or another aspect of His plan.

Throughout this journey, maintaining a sense of hope and expectation is vital. God's promises are steadfast, and His timing is impeccable. As we wait for the fulfillment of His promises, including the possibility of a future spouse, we can find solace in knowing that He is working on our behalf. Our role is to remain faithful, to trust in His plan, and to continue seeking His Kingdom and His righteousness.

Embracing our role as single women within the context of God's Kingdom involves recognizing the unique opportunities and responsibilities that come with this phase of life. By living out our faith, participating in the work of redemption, and aligning ourselves with God's governance and promises, we contribute to the expansion of His Kingdom. As we wait for His perfect timing and trust in His plan, we can find purpose and fulfillment in our current state, knowing that our lives are part of His grand design. Through our actions, prayers, and dedication, we engage in the ongoing work of God's Kingdom and reflect His love and grace to the world.

As I navigate through my journey of faith, I am continually reminded of the profound truth encapsulated in 2 Corinthians 1:20: "For all the promises of God in Him are yea, and in Him Amen, unto the glory of God by us." This scripture resonates deeply within me, affirming that everything I need from the universe is found in God's promises. The essence of this verse is a powerful declaration of divine provision, assurance, and fulfillment, highlighting that every promise God has made is both certain and complete in Christ.

In my walk with God, this verse has become a cornerstone of my faith, illustrating that God's promises are not just hopeful ideals but are assured realities. The phrase "For all the promises of God in Him are yea" signifies that every promise God has made is confirmed and fulfilled in Jesus Christ. It reassures me that nothing is left to chance, and nothing is outside the scope of God's sovereign plan. Every aspect of my life, every need, and every desire is encompassed within the promises God has made, and these promises are guaranteed by His unchanging nature.

This truth compels me to reflect on the nature of God's promises. They are not contingent on my actions or my perceived worthiness but are grounded in God's inherent faithfulness and grace. When I read "and in Him Amen," I understand that Christ is the ultimate affirmation of every promise. In Him, every divine pledge is validated and brought to fruition. This perspective helps me to approach life with a sense of confidence and security, knowing that my needs and aspirations are met not by my own efforts but through the abundant provision of God.

Moving forward in alignment with God's will is a continual process of trusting and relying on this promise. Each step I take is guided by the assurance that God's promises are active and operative in my life. As I face challenges or uncertainties, I remind myself that everything I need is already provided within the scope of God's promises. This understanding allows me to move forward with faith, even when the path is unclear or fraught with obstacles.

In practical terms, this means that when I encounter difficulties or when my plans seem to falter, I am encouraged to anchor my hope in God's promises rather than in my circumstances. The assurance that "all the promises of God" are reliable and fulfilled in Christ motivates me to persevere and to remain steadfast in my faith. I am reminded that my needs—whether they be spiritual, emotional, or physical—are fully addressed by God's promises.

This perspective also calls me to an active faith, one that involves not only believing in God's promises but also living in a manner that reflects my trust in them. Moving forward in God's will involves a daily commitment to align my thoughts, actions, and decisions with His divine guidance. I am encouraged to seek His will earnestly, to engage in prayer and study, and to cultivate a relationship with Him that is grounded in trust and obedience.

Furthermore, this understanding of God's promises provides a profound sense of peace and stability. Knowing that every promise is assured and that God's provision is complete in Christ helps me to remain calm in the face of uncertainty. I am able to navigate life with a sense of purpose and direction, confident that I am supported by the divine assurances that undergird my journey.

Embracing the fullness of 2 Corinthians 1:20 also means recognizing that God's promises extend beyond my immediate needs. They encompass His broader plan for my life and for the world. This realization inspires me to look beyond my personal circumstances and to consider how I can contribute to the fulfillment of God's promises in a larger context. Whether through acts of service, sharing the Gospel, or supporting others in their faith journeys, I am called to participate in the ongoing work of God's Kingdom.

As I continue to move forward in alignment with God's will, I am constantly reminded that His promises are not static but dynamic and active. They are working in my life, shaping my experiences, and guiding my steps. This dynamic aspect of God's promises encourages me to remain engaged and proactive in my faith, to seek out opportunities for growth, and to trust in His ongoing provision and guidance.

The profound truth of 2 Corinthians 1:20 offers a foundation of hope, assurance, and purpose. As I embrace the reality that everything I need from the universe is provided within the scope of God's promises, I am inspired to move forward with confidence and faith. Each promise is a testament to God's unwavering faithfulness and grace, and as I align my life with His will, I participate in the fulfillment of these divine assurances. Through this journey, I am reminded of the richness of God's provision and the profound impact of living a life anchored in His promises.

Instructions for a Single Woman

As I look into the profound message of Colossians 3:22, "Servants, obey in all things your masters according to the flesh; not with eyeservice, as men pleasers; but in singleness of heart, fearing God," I find a deep, transformative truth that speaks directly to the essence of how we live out our faith in practical terms. This scripture challenges me to examine my attitude and actions in every aspect of life, particularly in how I serve others and align my conduct with God's will. The verse calls me to a higher standard of service—one that goes beyond mere compliance and taps into the core of my relationship with God.

In reflecting on this verse, I am reminded that "servants" in this context refers to anyone who is in a position of service or submission, whether in a formal employment setting or in various other roles in life. It's a call to obey those in authority "according to the flesh," meaning in our earthly roles and responsibilities. For me, this means acknowledging the structures and hierarchies present in my life—be it at work, in my community, or even in personal relationships—and committing to fulfilling my duties with diligence and integrity. The call to obey "in all things" is not a mere suggestion but a command to approach every task and responsibility with a heart of commitment and respect.

However, Colossians 3:22 challenges me to go beyond outward appearances and perform my duties "not with eyeservice, as men pleasers." This phrase resonates deeply, reminding me that my service should not be merely about appearing to do the right thing when others are watching. It's easy to fall into the trap of performing for the approval of others, but this scripture calls me to a deeper authenticity. My actions are to be motivated by a genuine desire to honor God rather than seeking human praise or approval. This shift in motivation requires a heart transformation, where my primary focus becomes pleasing God rather than seeking the validation of those around me.

The core of this verse lies in the concept of "singleness of heart." For me, this means serving with a unified and undivided devotion. It involves aligning my inner attitudes and external actions so that they reflect a consistent commitment to God. This singleness of heart is about having a pure, undistracted focus in my service. It's an invitation to live with integrity, where my actions and intentions are harmoniously aligned with my faith. This unity of heart is not just about how I perform tasks but also about the underlying attitude with which I approach them.

The final part of the verse, "fearing God," encapsulates the ultimate motivation for my service. The "fear of God" here is not a fear of punishment but a deep reverence and respect for God's authority and holiness. This reverential fear inspires me to serve with a sense of awe and accountability to God. It is this fear that governs my behavior, ensuring that my service is done with a recognition of God's sovereignty and a desire to honor Him in every aspect of my life.

Living out this verse in practical terms involves a daily commitment to approach my roles and responsibilities with a heart that is fully engaged and devoted to God. It means checking my motives regularly to ensure that I am not merely performing for the sake of appearances but truly seeking to fulfill God's will through my service. This can be a challenging journey, as it requires constant self-reflection and a willingness to align my actions with God's standards.

In the context of singleness, this verse takes on an additional layer of meaning. Singleness offers a unique opportunity to focus on serving others with a heart aligned to God without the additional responsibilities that come with marriage or family life. It allows me to direct my energy and efforts toward serving with excellence and dedication, leveraging my time and resources for the glory of God. This period of singleness can be a time of intense personal growth and spiritual development, where I can cultivate a deeper relationship with God and a more refined approach to service.

As I strive to embody the principles of Colossians 3:22, I am continually reminded that my service is ultimately a reflection of my relationship with God. It's a call to live out my faith in tangible ways, demonstrating the transformative power of a heart dedicated to Him. The way I serve, whether in professional settings, personal interactions, or community involvement, becomes a testimony to the authenticity of my faith and my commitment to honoring God in all aspects of my life.

Colossians 3:22 provides a powerful framework for understanding and living out the essence of service from a place of divine alignment. As I embrace the call to serve with "singleness of heart" and to "fear God," I am continually challenged to examine my motivations, align my actions with my faith, and offer my service as an act of reverence and devotion. This journey is not only about fulfilling my responsibilities but also about reflecting the character of God through every aspect of my service. Through this commitment, I find a deeper sense of purpose and fulfillment, knowing that my service is a meaningful expression of my relationship with God and His will for my life.

Reflecting on 1 Samuel 15:22, which states, "To obey is better than sacrifice, and to hearken than the fat of rams," I am profoundly challenged to understand the true essence of obedience and its pivotal role in my spiritual life. This verse resonates deeply with me, emphasizing that God values obedience above ritualistic acts of worship or sacrifice. In the context of this scripture, I am called to examine how I submit to authority, adhere to God's Word, and align my heart with His expectations.

To obey in all things, as this verse instructs, requires me to approach my responsibilities and interactions with a genuine spirit of compliance and attentiveness. It's not about merely following orders or performing tasks for the sake of appearances, but about a deep-seated commitment to listening and responding with sincerity. This obedience is not superficial but is rooted in a respectful and mindful attitude toward those in authority and, more importantly, towards God Himself. It involves a conscious effort to be fully engaged and attentive to the guidance and expectations set before me.

In practical terms, this means submitting to authority with a heart that is open and willing, recognizing the roles and responsibilities I am entrusted with. It calls me to respect and admire the leadership and guidance provided, acknowledging that these roles are part of God's divine order. Whether it's in the workplace, in relationships, or within the community, this submission is a reflection of my commitment to aligning with God's will and purpose. It is a call to not only be compliant but to genuinely honor and uphold the standards set forth.

Moreover, being compliant and submitting to authority involves a readiness to listen and act upon the guidance provided. It requires a proactive attitude, where I am not just passively receiving instructions but actively engaging with them, ensuring that my actions reflect a thoughtful and considerate approach. This level of obedience is about being intelligent in my submission, understanding that my responsiveness is a key aspect of living out God's will.

Respecting and admiring the Holy Spirit, as mentioned, is crucial in this process. The Holy Spirit is my guide, providing wisdom and direction as I navigate the complexities of life. To honor the Holy Spirit is to acknowledge His role in guiding my decisions and actions, ensuring that I am in alignment with God's truth and purpose. This respect is not merely about external compliance but about cultivating a heart that is attuned to the Spirit's leading and responsive to His promptings.

As a servant, the call to obey in all things as my master according to the flesh and with a singleness of heart, while fearing God, highlights the importance of integrating my faith with my daily actions. It underscores the need for a cohesive and unified approach to living out my responsibilities, where my service reflects a deep reverence for God and a sincere commitment to fulfilling His will. Hearing the voice of God and responding with obedience is not just a matter of duty but an essential aspect of my spiritual journey.

Failing to obey, or disregarding God's guidance, is not a trivial matter. It signifies a disconnect from His purpose and a failure to honor the divine order He has established. It is a reminder that obedience is a fundamental aspect of my relationship with God and a key to experiencing His blessings and favor. This verse serves as a constant reminder to align my actions with God's expectations, ensuring that my service and submission are not just external acts but reflections of a heart that is fully devoted to Him.

In conclusion, 1 Samuel 15:22 challenges me to embrace obedience as a core value in my spiritual life. It calls me to submit to authority with sincerity, respect the guidance of the Holy Spirit, and integrate my faith with my daily actions. This obedience is not about mere compliance but about a deep, heartfelt commitment to living out God's will with integrity and reverence. As I strive to embody this principle, I am reminded of the profound impact of aligning my actions with God's expectations and the blessings that come from living a life of true obedience.

To obey Jehovah God is to embrace the divine wisdom and guidance that He offers us daily. This commitment to obedience requires me to exercise my faith in practical, everyday choices, ensuring that my actions and decisions align with His Word. God's instructions are not merely suggestions but divine truths that provide the foundation for a life lived in accordance with His will. By following these instructions diligently, I am participating in the larger mission of winning souls for the Kingdom of Heaven, contributing to the fulfillment of His divine plan.

Every day, I am presented with opportunities to practice obedience, whether in my interactions with others, my personal decisions, or my spiritual practices. Each moment is a chance to align myself with God's Word, to live out the principles He has laid out for us, and to reflect His character in my life. This exercise in obedience is not a burdensome task but a joyful privilege, as it allows me to grow closer to God and to fulfill the purpose He has set before me.

The truth of God's Word serves as a guiding light, illuminating the path I am to follow. By adhering to His instructions, I am not only ensuring my own alignment with His will but also contributing to the broader goal of expanding His Kingdom. This process of living out His Word empowers me to be a vessel through which others can see the love and truth of God. It enables me to be a part of His redemptive work, reaching out to those around me and drawing them closer to the hope and salvation found in Jesus Christ.

Standing firm in the truth of God's Word, I recognize that I am already prepared for the work He has called me to do. This preparation is not about acquiring new skills or knowledge but about fully embracing and utilizing the resources and gifts that God has already placed within me. As I remain steadfast and obedient, I am equipped to carry out His commands and to make a meaningful impact in the lives of others.

For singles, this understanding is particularly empowering. In this season of life, I have the opportunity to focus on my relationship with God and to be fully engaged in His work. I have all that I need to live out His commands and to contribute to the Kingdom. My singleness is not a limitation but a period of preparation and opportunity. It is a time to develop my spiritual strength, to grow in faith, and to be a beacon of God's love and truth to those around me.

In practical terms, exercising obedience means making daily choices that reflect God's Word and His will. It involves listening to His voice, responding to His guidance, and acting in ways that honor Him. This obedience is not always easy, but it is always worthwhile. It requires a commitment to living in alignment with His principles and a dedication to following His instructions, even when it challenges me or requires sacrifice.

As I continue to practice obedience, I am reminded that God's promises are true and His Word is reliable. He has promised to be with me, to guide me, and to empower me as I seek to fulfill His will. By trusting in His promises and remaining obedient to His Word, I am participating in His divine plan and contributing to the growth of His Kingdom.

To obey Jehovah God is to live out the truth of His Word with integrity and faithfulness. It involves exercising daily obedience, standing firm in His promises, and utilizing the gifts and resources He has provided. For singles, this season of life is an opportunity to be fully engaged in God's work and to contribute to His Kingdom with purpose and dedication. By embracing this call to obedience, I am aligning myself with God's will and participating in His redemptive work, impacting the lives of those around me and furthering His Kingdom on earth.

Spreading the gospel of Jesus Christ while faithfully following the instructions of the Lord is a fundamental aspect of my faith journey. I am deeply committed to sharing the message of salvation and grace with others, recognizing that this mission is not just a calling but a divine imperative. It requires more than mere outward compliance; it demands a sincere and heartfelt commitment to living out the truth of God's Word in every aspect of my life.

One of the key lessons I have learned is that serving others should never be done with "eye service." This concept, as outlined in Scripture, means that my service to others should not be motivated by the desire for recognition or praise from people. Instead, it should come from a genuine desire to honor God and to reflect His love and grace. Whether in my interactions with others or in my broader ministry efforts, my focus must remain on serving with a pure heart, dedicated to fulfilling God's will rather than seeking human approval.

In the pursuit of this mission, I am guided by the truth of 2 Corinthians 20:15, which reminds me not to be afraid. Fear can often be a significant obstacle when it comes to stepping out in faith and sharing the gospel. It may manifest as a fear of rejection, failure, or even opposition. However, I am assured by this Scripture that fear should not deter me from carrying out my divine responsibilities. Instead, I am encouraged to trust in God's sovereignty and to move forward with confidence, knowing that He is with me every step of the way.

The essence of my service and witness is to be rooted in the truth of God's Word and to be characterized by authenticity and dedication. This means that my actions, words, and motivations should align with the teachings of Jesus Christ. By following His example, I strive to demonstrate love, compassion, and integrity in all that I do. This commitment involves being attentive to God's instructions, seeking His guidance through prayer, and being obedient to His call.

Moreover, spreading the gospel involves more than just verbal proclamation; it requires living out the principles of the faith in practical ways. This might include acts of kindness, support for those in need, and a willingness to engage in conversations about faith with those who are seeking answers. My service should reflect the transformative power of the gospel, showing others what it means to live a life transformed by Christ.

As I engage in this mission, I am also reminded of the importance of perseverance. The journey of spreading the gospel is not always straightforward or easy. There may be challenges, setbacks, and moments of doubt. However, I am encouraged by the promise that God is faithful and will provide the strength and wisdom needed to overcome these obstacles. By remaining steadfast in my commitment and trusting in His guidance, I can continue to faithfully share the message of Jesus Christ.

In practical terms, this means that I must be proactive in seeking opportunities to share the gospel. Whether through personal relationships, community involvement, or outreach initiatives, I am called to be an active participant in the work of God's Kingdom. This involves being prepared to give an answer for the hope that I have, to offer encouragement and support to others, and to be a living testament to the power of God's grace.

Ultimately, spreading the gospel and following God's instructions requires a heart that is fully devoted to Him. It involves embracing the truth of His Word, living out His commands, and trusting in His promises. As I continue to follow this path, I am committed to serving with authenticity, overcoming fear, and remaining dedicated to the mission of sharing the gospel of Jesus Christ with others. Through this journey, I am not only fulfilling my calling but also contributing to the expansion of God's Kingdom and the fulfillment of His divine plan.

The battle is not ours; it is the Lord's. This profound truth has become a cornerstone of my faith and understanding as I navigate the challenges and trials of life. When I am faced with difficulties, conflicts, or uncertainties, I am reminded that I do not need to bear the burden alone. The battle belongs to God, and He is sovereign over all circumstances. This realization brings me a deep sense of peace and reassurance, knowing that my role is not to fight the battle in my own strength, but to trust in God's power and wisdom.

In moments of fear or dismay, especially when confronted by people or situations that seem overwhelming, I am encouraged by the promise that I have already won the battle through Christ. It is not about whether I can overcome every challenge on my own, but about recognizing that victory has already been secured through Jesus' sacrifice and resurrection. This victory is a profound and unshakable truth that empowers me to face life's struggles with confidence and hope.

Following God's Word and His instructions is crucial to living out this truth. John 8:32 states, "Ye shall know the truth, and the truth shall make you free." This verse is a powerful reminder that knowing and embracing God's truth is the key to freedom and victory in our lives. When I immerse myself in the Scriptures, I am not just reading historical accounts or moral teachings; I am engaging with the living Word of God, which has the power to transform and liberate.

To "know the truth" means to have a deep, personal understanding of God's Word and to apply it to every aspect of my life. This knowledge is not merely intellectual; it is experiential and relational. It involves a genuine relationship with God, characterized by obedience, faith, and trust. As I follow His instructions and align my life with His truth, I am empowered to live in the freedom that He provides.

God's truth offers a foundation of stability and assurance in a world that is often chaotic and uncertain. When I know the truth of His promises, I can stand firm in my faith, even in the face of adversity. This truth gives me the strength to overcome fear, to resist temptation, and to remain steadfast in my commitment to His ways. It also helps me to navigate relationships and situations with wisdom and grace, knowing that God's truth guides me in making choices that honor Him.

Furthermore, knowing the truth of God's Word equips me to be an effective witness to others. As I live out the freedom and transformation that comes from embracing His truth, I can share this message with those around me. My life becomes a testimony to the power of God's Word, demonstrating how His truth has brought freedom, healing, and renewal. This witness is not just about sharing Scripture but about embodying the principles of God's kingdom in a way that attracts others to His grace and love.

In practical terms, following God's Word involves daily devotion, prayer, and reflection. It requires a commitment to studying the Scriptures, seeking His guidance, and applying His principles to everyday life. It also means being responsive to His voice and obedient to His leading, even when it challenges my comfort or expectations. By doing so, I remain aligned with His will and experience the fullness of the freedom and victory that He offers.

Ultimately, embracing the truth of God's Word is about living in the reality of His promises and His power. It is about recognizing that He is in control, that His victory is assured, and that I am called to live in that victory. As I continue to follow His instructions and trust in His truth, I am confident that I am fulfilling my role in His divine plan and experiencing the abundant life that He has promised.

In summary, the battle is the Lord's, and I am assured of victory through Him. By knowing and living according to His truth, I am free from fear and empowered to face life's challenges with confidence. This understanding shapes my daily life, guiding me in my actions, decisions, and relationships. As I embrace His Word and follow His instructions, I am fully equipped to live out the victory that Christ has secured and to share this message of hope and freedom with others.

God has set His purpose on my life, and this profound truth fills me with awe and gratitude. Psalm 37:5 states, "Commit your way to the Lord; trust also in Him, and He shall bring it to pass." This verse serves as a powerful reminder of the divine purpose and plan that God has uniquely crafted for each of us. When I reflect on this Scripture, I am reassured that my life is not a series of random events or unplanned occurrences but a carefully orchestrated journey by God Himself.

Understanding that God has set His purpose on my life gives me a sense of direction and clarity. It means that my steps are guided by His wisdom and that every aspect of my life is under His sovereign control. This realization transforms how I approach each day, knowing that my actions, decisions, and even my challenges are part of a larger, divine plan. It encourages me to align my goals and aspirations with His will, trusting that He is working all things together for good.

As I commit my way to the Lord and trust in Him, I am also participating in a greater mission. My life, shaped by His purpose, becomes a vessel through which His love and truth can be shared with others. This purpose is not just about personal fulfillment or success but about contributing to the expansion of His Kingdom. I am called to be an instrument of His grace, using my gifts and experiences to draw others closer to Him.

The knowledge that my life is purposeful also empowers me to face challenges with a sense of hope and perseverance. Even when things don't go as planned or when I encounter obstacles, I can trust that these experiences are part of God's plan to fulfill His purpose in my life. This trust enables me to remain steadfast and resilient, knowing that God's purposes are being accomplished even in the midst of difficulties.

Moreover, recognizing that God's purpose for my life can bring souls to His Kingdom is both humbling and motivating. It means that my life and witness can have a significant impact on others, leading them to experience the love and salvation of Jesus Christ. This perspective shifts my focus from merely seeking personal gain to being an active participant in the Great Commission. My daily interactions, decisions, and conversations become opportunities to reflect Christ's love and to share the message of hope with those around me.

In practical terms, living out this purpose involves a commitment to spiritual growth and alignment with God's will. It requires daily prayer, studying His Word, and seeking His guidance in every aspect of life. By remaining close to Him and trusting in His plan, I am better equipped to fulfill the purpose He has set for me. This involves being open to His leading, willing to step out in faith, and ready to serve others in ways that reflect His character and grace.

Ultimately, knowing that God has set His purpose in my life reassures me of my worth and significance in His grand design. It inspires me to live with intention and to seek opportunities to be a blessing to others. As I commit my way to the Lord and trust in Him, I am confident that He will bring His purpose to fruition, and that my life will bear fruit for His Kingdom. This understanding guides me in my daily walk, shapes my interactions with others, and fuels my desire to be a faithful and effective ambassador for Christ.

I trust deeply in the knowledge that God understands my desires, including my longing for marriage. This assurance brings me comfort and hope, knowing that my desires are not overlooked or dismissed by the Lord. Proverbs 3:5-6 says, "Trust in the Lord with all thine heart; and lean not unto thine own understanding. In all thy ways acknowledge Him, and He shall direct thy paths." This Scripture is a cornerstone of my faith journey, reminding me to place my complete trust in God, even when my heart yearns for something as significant as marriage.

Understanding that God knows my desires and has a plan for my life encourages me to embrace a purposeful mindset. It is easy to become consumed by the longing for companionship and to focus solely on what I don't yet have. However, this verse calls me to redirect my focus from my own understanding to a broader, divine perspective. I am encouraged to trust in God's timing and His plan for my life, believing that He is guiding me toward what is best.

By trusting in the Lord with all my heart, I commit to surrendering my desires and plans to Him. I recognize that my understanding is limited compared to His infinite wisdom. There are times when I may not fully grasp why certain things are happening or why my desires have not yet been fulfilled. Yet, I am reminded that God's ways are higher than mine, and His understanding surpasses all. This trust allows me to find peace in the midst of uncertainty, knowing that He is orchestrating every detail of my life according to His perfect will.

In the midst of waiting and trusting, I am also called to be purposeful in my journey. The desire for marriage is not merely a personal longing but an opportunity to reflect on how I can serve and impact others while I wait. I am reminded that my life is not on hold but rather a continual unfolding of God's purpose. This perspective shifts my focus from waiting passively to actively engaging in the work of the Kingdom.

Becoming a purposeful woman involves more than simply waiting for a future spouse. It means actively living out my faith and making a positive impact in the lives of others. By focusing on winning souls for the Kingdom of God, I align my efforts with a higher calling. My purpose is to share the love and truth of Jesus Christ, to be a light in the world, and to contribute to the growth of His Kingdom.

Each day presents opportunities to be intentional in my actions and interactions. Whether it is through serving others, sharing the Gospel, or living out the values of Christ, I am committed to making a difference. This purposeful living is not confined to any particular phase of life but is a continuous journey of faith and obedience. By focusing on these aspects, I transform my desire for marriage into a broader mission of serving and impacting others for God's glory.

I also recognize that being purposeful involves personal growth and preparation. This time of singleness is an opportunity for me to develop qualities that will benefit not only my future marriage but also my current service to God. It is a period of learning, growing, and becoming the person God has called me to be. As I invest in my spiritual growth, develop my character, and cultivate a heart of service, I prepare myself to be a more effective witness and a more loving partner in the future.

Furthermore, I am reminded that my purpose is deeply intertwined with God's greater plan. He has a unique and specific plan for my life, including the desires of my heart. Trusting in Him means believing that His timing is perfect and that He is working all things together for my good. Even as I pursue my purpose and strive to win souls for His Kingdom, I hold on to the promise that He is at work in every aspect of my life, including my desire for marriage.

In conclusion, trusting in the Lord with all my heart while remaining purposeful in my journey allows me to align my desires with God's plan. By focusing on serving others and advancing His Kingdom, I embrace a life of purpose that transcends personal longing. This trust and purpose transform my journey of singleness into an active and fulfilling path, knowing that God is guiding me, preparing me, and ultimately fulfilling His plan for my life.

In the journey of singleness, I have come to understand that finding peace and fulfillment is deeply intertwined with embracing God's Word and His plan for my life. As a woman navigating this season, I have learned that true contentment does not come from seeking a future spouse or achieving societal milestones but from aligning my heart with God's purpose and trusting in His timing.

God's Word provides profound guidance on how to approach singleness. Proverbs 3:5-6 has been a cornerstone for me, reminding me to "Trust in the Lord with all thine heart; and lean not unto thine own understanding. In all thy ways acknowledge Him, and He shall direct thy paths." This Scripture encourages me to place my trust completely in God, even when my desires and understanding might lead me to question His timing. Trusting in God means accepting that His plans for me are perfect, even if they differ from my own expectations.

In this phase of life, finding peace starts with recognizing that my value and purpose are not contingent on marital status. God has set a purpose for my life that extends beyond the realm of relationships. Embracing this purpose means focusing on how I can serve others, grow spiritually, and impact the Kingdom of God. My time of singleness is an opportunity to deepen my relationship with God, to understand His Word more profoundly, and to prepare myself to fulfill the role He has for me.

Being purposeful in singleness involves actively living out my faith and making a difference in the lives of others. It means not waiting passively for the future but engaging in the work of God's Kingdom right now. By focusing on sharing the Gospel, serving others, and living according to Christ's teachings, I contribute to the expansion of His Kingdom and find fulfillment in my current state.

Personal growth is another crucial aspect of this journey. Singleness offers a unique opportunity for self-improvement and spiritual development. As I invest in my character, deepen my spiritual practices, and cultivate a heart of service, I am preparing myself for whatever God has in store for me, whether that includes future marriage or a continued focus on ministry and personal growth.

Moreover, understanding that God's plan for me is perfect and His timing is impeccable helps to alleviate the anxiety and restlessness that can accompany singleness. I remind myself that God knows the desires of my heart and that He is working all things together for my good. This assurance allows me to find peace and contentment in the present, trusting that God's plan will unfold in His perfect time.

Ultimately, finding peace in singleness requires a shift in focus from what I lack to what I can give. It involves aligning my desires with God's purpose and trusting Him fully. As I concentrate on living out His Word, serving others, and growing spiritually, I discover that true peace comes from embracing my current state with joy and purpose. This journey is about more than waiting for the future; it is about living fully and faithfully in the present, knowing that God is with me every step of the way.

Purpose of the Single Woman Is to Obey God

As I reflect on Ephesians 6:5-9, I am profoundly moved by the depth and clarity of the instructions given to me about how to conduct myself in various aspects of life. This passage challenges me to examine not only my actions but also the motives behind them, urging me to approach my responsibilities with a heart of sincerity and dedication.

Verse 5 of Ephesians 6 speaks directly to my role and responsibilities: "Servants, be obedient to them that are your masters according to the flesh, with fear and trembling, in the singleness of your heart, as unto Christ." This instruction resonates deeply with me as it emphasizes the need for obedience and respect in my interactions, particularly in roles where I am accountable to others. The phrase "with fear and trembling" does not suggest a paralyzing fear but rather an attitude of reverence and seriousness towards the duties I am entrusted with. It calls me to approach my responsibilities with a sense of gravity and respect, recognizing that my service is ultimately an act of devotion to Christ.

The passage continues with a crucial admonition: "Not with eyeservice, as men-pleasers." This part of the verse hits home for me, as it challenges me to evaluate my motivations. It's easy to slip into the habit of performing tasks with the intention of seeking approval or recognition from others. However, this verse calls me to rise above mere appearances and to work diligently and honestly, not just when people are watching but consistently, regardless of external validation. It reminds me that my true audience is God, and my work should be a reflection of my commitment to Him, rather than an effort to impress those around me.

In verses 6 and 7, I am encouraged to serve "with good will, as to the Lord, and not to men." This directive is transformative for me, as it shifts my focus from seeking human approval to aiming to please God in all that I do. It challenges me to align my work ethic and attitudes with God's will, embodying His love and grace in my daily actions. This perspective helps me view my responsibilities as opportunities to honor God, turning routine tasks into acts of worship.

Verse 9 addresses those in positions of authority: "And ye, masters, do the same things unto them, forbearing threatening: knowing that your Master also is in heaven; neither is there respect of persons with him." This instruction underscores the principle of mutual respect and fairness. It reminds me that regardless of my position, whether as a leader or a follower, the ultimate authority is God, who treats everyone with impartiality. It challenges me to treat others with fairness, compassion, and integrity, recognizing that my actions are ultimately accountable to God.

Applying this passage to my life, I see a profound call to integrity and authenticity. I am reminded that my service and interactions are not merely about fulfilling obligations or gaining approval but about reflecting my devotion to Christ in every aspect of my life. This passage challenges me to cultivate a heart of genuine dedication and to approach my responsibilities with a sincere commitment to honor God. Whether in professional settings, personal relationships, or everyday tasks, I am called to act with integrity, recognizing that my true reward comes from God, who sees and values the sincerity of my heart.

In practical terms, this means examining my motives and ensuring that my actions are not driven by a desire for external validation but by a genuine desire to serve God. It involves being honest and diligent in all that I do, approaching my responsibilities with a sense of reverence and dedication. By focusing on serving Christ rather than seeking human approval, I am empowered to live with authenticity and purpose, transforming my approach to work and relationships.

Overall, Ephesians 6:5-9 offers a profound blueprint for living with integrity and dedication. It challenges me to serve with sincerity, to view my responsibilities as acts of worship, and to treat others with respect and fairness. By embracing these principles, I can align my life more closely with God's will, reflecting His love and grace in all that I do.

As I delve into the profound truth that "according to the flesh" refers to the outer aspects of our being, I am struck by the contrast between how humans and God perceive us. This distinction is central to understanding not just how we should view ourselves, but also how we should approach our interactions with others. The outer part—the physical appearance, the way we present ourselves, and the outward behavior—is often what people focus on. This is the part that attracts attention and often dictates how we are judged and valued in society. Yet, it's vital for me to remember that this is not the entirety of who we are.

For as long as I can remember, I have been aware of how people are often preoccupied with external appearances. Whether it's the clothes we wear, our physical attributes, or our mannerisms, society places a significant emphasis on these visible traits. It's easy to fall into the trap of believing that our worth and the worth of others are measured by these external factors. I have often found myself caught in this cycle, where I judge others based on their outward appearance and am, in turn, judged by my own.

However, as I reflect on God's perspective, I am reminded of a powerful truth: God looks at the heart. This divine view challenges me to look beyond superficial judgments and to recognize the true essence of a person. When God sees us, He does not merely observe the outer shell; He discerns our innermost thoughts, intentions, and desires. This realization is both humbling and liberating. It means that no matter how we might be judged by human standards, our true value and worth are determined by our hearts and our relationship with God.

In 1 Samuel 16:7, we are reminded that "man looks at the outward appearance, but the Lord looks at the heart." This passage is a constant reminder to me that the external aspects of our lives, while important in the eyes of society, are not the ultimate measure of our worth. God's judgment is based on the purity of our hearts, our intentions, and our faithfulness. This understanding calls me to evaluate how I perceive and interact with others.

If I am to embody Christ's love and perspective, I must strive to see others through His eyes. This means looking beyond physical appearances and recognizing the intrinsic worth and potential within each person. It requires me to approach others with empathy and compassion, understanding that their value is not dictated by how they look or how they present themselves, but by their hearts and their relationship with God.

In practical terms, this understanding has profound implications for my daily life. It challenges me to interact with others not based on their outward appearance or societal status but on the content of their character and the sincerity of their hearts. It calls me to cultivate a heart of genuine love and acceptance, viewing others with the same grace and understanding that Christ extends to me.

Furthermore, this perspective affects how I view myself. It means that I should not place undue emphasis on my external appearance or achievements but focus instead on cultivating a heart that is aligned with God's will. It invites me to seek inner growth and spiritual development, knowing that my true worth is found in my relationship with God and the state of my heart.

The challenge is to maintain this perspective in a world that continually emphasizes superficial values. Everywhere I turn, there are messages about physical perfection, material success, and social status. These external factors are often highlighted as the ultimate measures of success and worth. Yet, by focusing on God's view, I am reminded that these external metrics are fleeting and secondary to the eternal value of the heart.

As I strive to see others as God sees them, I also recognize the importance of extending this perspective to myself. It's easy to become preoccupied with personal insecurities and societal pressures, but God's view reminds me of my inherent worth and the importance of nurturing my inner self. This understanding encourages me to invest in my spiritual growth, to develop qualities such as kindness, humility, and faithfulness, and to focus on living a life that reflects God's love and purpose.

Ultimately, embracing this perspective involves a shift from valuing external appearances to valuing the heart and character. It's about recognizing that our worth is not defined by how we look or how others perceive us but by our relationship with God and our faithfulness to His commands. It's about living in a way that honors God, reflecting His love to others, and nurturing a heart that is aligned with His will.

This perspective is not just a personal challenge but a call to action. It's about transforming how I view others and myself, allowing God's perspective to shape my interactions and my sense of self-worth. It's about fostering a community where people are valued for who they are in Christ, where the heart is honored above the outward appearance, and where love and grace prevail.

The call to view others and myself through the lens of God's heart rather than the fleshly external is both a profound and practical challenge. It invites me to align my perceptions with God's, to focus on inner character rather than outward appearances, and to live in a way that reflects His love and grace. By doing so, I can contribute to a world where true value is recognized, and every person is honored for their intrinsic worth and relationship with God.

As I ponder the divine call to service and the obligation that comes with it, I am deeply moved by the realization that the Lord is indeed calling me to serve and fulfill the unique purpose He has set before me. This call is not just an invitation but a profound obligation that requires my full dedication and commitment. I am constantly reminded that to follow God is to embrace a life of service, where obedience and leadership are intertwined with my faith journey. The weight of this responsibility is both humbling and empowering, as I recognize that my role in God's plan is not one of passive acceptance but active participation.

In reflecting on my calling, I understand that service to the Lord is not merely about performing tasks or fulfilling duties; it is about aligning my heart with His will and dedicating myself to His purposes. This calling encompasses every aspect of my life, urging me to lead by example, to live in a manner that honors Him, and to actively engage in the work He has set before me. The obligation to serve is not a burden but a privilege, one that comes with the promise of fulfillment and purpose. By dedicating myself to this calling, I become a vessel through which God's love, grace, and truth can be manifested in the world.

To lead and obey as God has called me involves a deep commitment to understanding His will and following His guidance. It means that I must continually seek His direction through prayer, study of His Word, and listening to His voice. This journey of obedience requires me to set aside my own desires and ambitions in favor of His plans. It challenges me to embrace a posture of humility and trust, recognizing that His ways are higher than my ways and His thoughts higher than my thoughts. In this process, I am called to surrender my will to His, allowing His purpose to take precedence over my own.

The call to serve and obey is also a call to leadership. As I take on this role, I must be mindful of the example I set for others. Leadership in the context of God's calling is not about exerting authority or seeking personal gain; it is about guiding others with integrity, compassion, and a steadfast commitment to His truth. I am reminded that my leadership should reflect the character of Christ—one that is marked by love, humility, and a genuine desire to see others grow in their faith. This kind of leadership requires me to be attentive to the needs of those I serve, to offer support and encouragement, and to foster an environment where God's purposes can flourish.

Obeying God's call means more than just following a set of instructions; it involves a deep, personal relationship with Him. It requires me to be attuned to His voice and responsive to His promptings. This obedience is a daily choice, one that involves setting aside my own preferences and aligning myself with His will. It is a journey that involves continuous growth and learning, as I seek to understand more fully the depths of His love and the breadth of His plans for me. In this process, I am called to remain steadfast and faithful, even when faced with challenges or uncertainties.

As I embrace this call to service and obedience, I am also aware of the impact it has on my own spiritual growth. Serving others and leading with integrity are opportunities for me to deepen my relationship with God and to grow in my faith. Each act of service and each step of obedience is a chance for me to experience His grace more fully and to witness the unfolding of His plans in my life. This journey is not just about fulfilling a duty but about growing closer to Him and becoming more aligned with His purpose.

The commitment to serve and obey is a reflection of my desire to honor God with my life. It is a response to His love and grace, acknowledging that all I have and all I am belong to Him. This understanding motivates me to live a life that is centered on His will and dedicated to His purposes. By serving with a heart of gratitude and obedience, I demonstrate my trust in His goodness and my commitment to His Kingdom.

In practical terms, this calling requires me to be proactive in seeking out opportunities for service and to be diligent in fulfilling the responsibilities entrusted to me. It means that I must be willing to step out of my comfort zone, to take risks for the sake of His Kingdom, and to persevere in the face of obstacles. This journey involves both the triumphs and the trials, but through it all, I am assured of His faithfulness and His presence.

Ultimately, the call to service and obedience is a call to live a life that is wholly devoted to God. It is a call to embrace the role He has designed for me and to fulfill it with excellence and dedication. By answering this call, I participate in the broader narrative of His redemptive work, contributing to the advancement of His Kingdom and the transformation of the world around me. This journey is a testament to His grace and a reflection of His love, and it is a privilege that I embrace with a full and open heart.

In conclusion, the call to serve and obey is a profound and transformative journey. It is an invitation to align my life with God's will, to lead with integrity, and to fulfill the responsibilities He has entrusted to me. By dedicating myself to this calling, I become a vessel for His purposes and a witness to His grace. This journey requires commitment, humility, and a deep trust in His plans, and it is a path that leads to both personal growth and the advancement of His Kingdom. As I answer this call, I do so with a heart full of gratitude and a commitment to serving Him with all that I am.

As I reflect on my journey of cohabitation with God, I am deeply moved by the profound reality of walking and thinking in the Spirit of Christ. This spiritual cohabitation is not merely a concept but a living, dynamic relationship with the Divine that shapes every aspect of my existence. To cohabit with God means to be so entwined with His presence that every thought, action, and decision is influenced by His Spirit. This is an intimate and ongoing interaction where His Spirit pervades my being, guiding me in every moment and aligning my life with His will.

Cohabitation with God starts with the acknowledgment of His omnipresence and His active involvement in my daily life. It is about recognizing that He is not a distant deity but a close, personal companion who desires to dwell within me and walk alongside me. This relationship is grounded in the indwelling of the Holy Spirit, who transforms my mind and heart to reflect the nature of Christ. Walking in the Spirit involves a conscious choice to align my thoughts and actions with the teachings of Jesus, allowing His Spirit to lead and guide me in all circumstances.

To walk in the Spirit of Christ means to let His values and principles govern my behavior. It involves embracing His love, compassion, and humility in my interactions with others. By thinking in the Spirit, I allow my mindset to be shaped by His teachings, focusing on spiritual growth, righteousness, and a deepening relationship with God. This transformation is not something I achieve on my own but through the continuous work of the Holy Spirit in my life. The Spirit renews my mind, refines my character, and empowers me to live according to God's will.

The concept of obedience is central to this journey of cohabitation with God. To be obedient is to adhere to God's commands and to live in alignment with His will. Obedience is not a mere act of compliance but a reflection of a heart fully devoted to God. It involves a willingness to listen to His voice, to follow His guidance, and to submit to His authority in every aspect of life. In essence, obedience is about recognizing God's sovereignty and responding with trust and faithfulness.

In my journey, I understand that being a servant of God means being obedient to Him in all things. This obedience is expressed through my daily actions, choices, and attitudes. It requires a surrender of my own desires and ambitions in favor of His plans and purposes. As a servant, my role is to faithfully carry out the responsibilities entrusted to me, to honor God through my actions, and to reflect His character in all that I do.

The term "obedience" encompasses several key aspects:

1. **Listening**: Obedience begins with a receptive ear. It involves hearing God's commands and understanding His will as revealed through Scripture, prayer, and the guidance of the Holy Spirit.

2. **Submission**: This aspect of obedience involves a willingness to align my actions with God's directives, even when it requires sacrifice or goes against my own preferences.

3. **Faithfulness**: Obedience is marked by a consistent and unwavering commitment to follow God's guidance, regardless of circumstances or challenges.

4. **Action**: True obedience manifests in actions that reflect God's commands. It is not merely about internal assent but about translating faith into tangible behaviors that honor Him.

5. **Respect**: Obedience involves a deep respect for God's authority and a recognition of His wisdom and righteousness.

In practical terms, obedience as a servant of God means living out His commands in every aspect of life. It means striving to love others as Christ loves, to act justly, and to walk humbly with God. This obedience is not always easy, but it is a testament to my commitment to God's kingdom and His purposes. By adhering to His commands, I demonstrate my trust in His wisdom and my dedication to living a life that reflects His character.

To cohabit with God and to be obedient requires a continual process of growth and renewal. It involves regularly seeking His guidance, repenting of my shortcomings, and striving to align my life with His will. This process is supported by regular prayer, Bible study, and fellowship with other believers. It is a journey that calls for perseverance and dedication, but it is also one that brings immense joy and fulfillment as I grow closer to God and fulfill His purposes for my life.

The essence of living in the Spirit of Christ and being obedient is to allow God's presence to transform me from the inside out. It is to live with an awareness of His constant presence and to let His Spirit guide every thought, word, and action. This journey is one of continuous growth and transformation, where each day offers new opportunities to deepen my relationship with God and to live out His commands in a way that honors Him.

Cohabitation with God is about embracing a life that is fully immersed in His Spirit and aligned with His will. It involves walking in the Spirit of Christ, being obedient to His commands, and reflecting His character in all that I do. As I continue to grow in this relationship, I am continually reminded of the importance of surrendering my will to His, listening to His voice, and living out His commands with faithfulness and integrity. This journey of obedience and cohabitation is both a privilege and a responsibility, and it is one that I embrace with a heart full of gratitude and dedication.

As I delve into the profound truth of serving God with "fear and trembling," I am constantly reminded of the deep reverence and respect that this phrase embodies. To love God, in its truest sense, involves a profound sense of awe and respect for His majesty and authority. The idea of "fear and trembling" is not about living in terror, but rather about approaching God with a heart full of reverence and humility, recognizing His infinite power and our own need for His guidance.

The fear of the Lord is indeed the beginning of wisdom, as Scripture reveals. This is not a fear that paralyzes or causes us to retreat in dread, but a fear that inspires a deep sense of wonder and respect for the Creator of the universe. It is through this reverence that we come to understand the true nature of wisdom and knowledge. When we acknowledge God's supreme authority and our own position in relation to Him, we open ourselves up to His teachings and His guidance. This reverence for God is the foundation upon which true wisdom is built, as it aligns our hearts and minds with His divine purpose.

Trembling, in this context, represents both a physical and emotional response to the profound reality of God's presence. Physically, it may manifest as a palpable reaction to the overwhelming sense of His power and majesty. Emotionally, it reflects the deep humility and awe that we feel when we stand in the presence of such a mighty and loving God. This trembling is not a sign of weakness but a testament to the depth of our reverence and the sincerity of our worship.

As I reflect on my own journey of faith, I realize that embracing this concept of fear and trembling has profoundly shaped my relationship with God. It has led me to approach Him with a heart that is both open and expectant, eager to receive His wisdom and to align my life with His will. This attitude of reverence transforms the way I live and interact with others, guiding me to act with integrity, compassion, and humility.

In my daily life, this reverence influences how I approach challenges and opportunities. When faced with difficult decisions, I find myself seeking God's guidance with a heart full of awe and a desire to honor Him in all things. This approach ensures that my actions are aligned with His will and that I am continually growing in wisdom and understanding. It is through this process that I learn to navigate life with greater clarity and purpose, recognizing that my ultimate goal is to live in a manner that reflects His love and truth.

Moreover, this understanding of fear and trembling deepens my appreciation for the role of the Holy Spirit in my life. The Spirit acts as a guide, helping me to understand and apply the principles of God's

Word with wisdom and discernment. This guidance is essential for living a life that honors God and fulfills His purposes for me. As I embrace this guidance, I am able to make choices that reflect His character and advance His kingdom on earth.

In essence, living with fear and trembling means allowing God's presence to profoundly impact every aspect of my life. It involves recognizing His sovereignty, seeking His wisdom, and responding to His call with a heart full of reverence and love. This approach not only shapes my personal spiritual journey but also influences how I engage with others and fulfill my role within the broader community of faith.

As I continue to grow in my understanding of what it means to serve God with fear and trembling, I am reminded of the importance of maintaining a posture of humility and openness. This attitude allows me to remain receptive to His teachings and to live in a way that reflects His love and grace. It is through this ongoing process of reverence and submission that I am able to live a life that truly honors Him and contributes to His purposes in the world.

In conclusion, the concept of serving God with fear and trembling is a profound and transformative aspect of the Christian faith. It calls us to approach God with deep respect and humility, recognizing His majesty and our need for His guidance. By embracing this attitude, we open ourselves to His wisdom and understanding, allowing His presence to shape our lives and guide our actions. This journey of reverence and submission is not only a path to personal growth but also a means of fulfilling our divine purpose and reflecting His love to those around us.

As I immerse myself in the profound message of John 14:27, I am continually moved by the depth of Jesus's promise of peace. He says, "Peace I leave with you; my peace I give unto you: not as the world giveth, give I unto you. Let not your heart be troubled, neither let it be afraid." These words resonate deeply within me, offering a reassurance that transcends the superficial calm that the world often offers. The peace that Jesus provides is a profound, unwavering peace that permeates every aspect of my life, a peace that cannot be disturbed by external circumstances or internal anxieties. This divine peace is a gift that I hold dear, for it is a reflection of the trust and confidence that I place in God's plan for my life.

Embracing this peace, I am called to serve as unto the Lord, working for Him with a heart full of dedication and commitment. This service is not merely about fulfilling tasks or meeting expectations; it is about aligning my actions with the divine will of God. As I serve, I am reminded that I am working not for human masters but for the Master Himself. This perspective transforms my approach to every task, infusing it with purpose and significance. The work I do becomes an act of worship, a way of honoring God and contributing to His greater plan.

The call to serve the Lord involves doing His will from the heart. This means that my service is not just about outward compliance but about an internal alignment with His desires. I am called to act out of genuine love and devotion, ensuring that my actions reflect the true nature of God's will. This service is an expression of my commitment to His purposes and a demonstration of my willingness to be used by Him in fulfilling His divine plan. It is through this heartfelt obedience that I find true fulfillment and purpose, knowing that my efforts are contributing to something far greater than myself.

In practicing this form of service, I am guided by the principles laid out in Scripture, particularly the idea of serving with a heart full of peace and dedication. The peace that Jesus promises is not just a comfort but a driving force that empowers me to serve with integrity and joy. It helps me to overcome challenges and difficulties, knowing that my efforts are aligned with His will and that He is with me every step of the way.

I recognize that true service to the Lord requires a surrender of my own will and desires in favor of His. This surrender is not always easy, as it often involves setting aside personal ambitions and preferences in favor of what God has planned. However, I find that this act of surrender brings me closer to Him and aligns my life more closely with His purposes. It is through this alignment that I experience a deeper sense of peace and satisfaction, knowing that I am fulfilling my role in His grand design.

Moreover, as I serve with this mindset, I become a vessel through which God's love and grace can flow to others. My actions, guided by His peace and purpose, become a testament to His goodness and faithfulness. This is not about seeking recognition or approval from others but about being a reflection of His character and demonstrating His love in tangible ways. It is in this service that I find a deeper connection with Him and a greater sense of joy and fulfillment.

The promise of peace that Jesus gives is a reminder that, even in the midst of challenges and uncertainties, I can remain steadfast and assured in my service to the Lord. This peace guards my heart and mind, helping me to remain focused on His will and to trust in His guidance. It allows me to navigate difficulties with grace and resilience, knowing that He is in control and that His plan is perfect.

John 14:27 offers a profound and transformative promise of peace that empowers and sustains me in my service to the Lord. By embracing this peace and aligning my actions with His will, I am able to serve with a heart full of dedication and purpose. This service becomes an act of worship and a reflection of my commitment to His divine plan. As I continue to live out this calling, I find a deeper sense of fulfillment and connection with God, knowing that my efforts are contributing to His greater work in the world.

Living a life that pleases God is the ultimate aspiration and guide for my daily existence. Each day, I am reminded that everything I do should be an act of worship and an expression of my commitment to Him. This concept is not merely a set of rules or a checklist but a profound and personal journey of aligning my actions, thoughts, and intentions with God's will.

At the heart of living to please God is a deep understanding of His nature and His desires for me. The Scriptures are my roadmap, providing clear guidance on how to live in a way that honors Him. For instance, in 1 Thessalonians 4:1, Paul exhorts us to "walk in a manner worthy of the Lord, fully pleasing to Him." This directive underscores that our daily actions should reflect His values and principles. By immersing myself in His Word, I gain insight into how to embody His teachings in every aspect of my life.

Living to please God requires more than just outward compliance; it demands a transformation of the heart. It is about cultivating a mindset that consistently seeks to reflect His love, grace, and truth. I strive to ensure that my actions are motivated by a genuine desire to honor Him rather than seeking personal gain or recognition. This involves setting aside my own preferences and aligning my desires with His will, trusting that His plans are always for my good.

A key aspect of pleasing God is walking in obedience to His commands. This obedience is not a mere duty but a heartfelt response to His love and grace. It means following His teachings even when it is challenging or counter-cultural. Through obedience, I demonstrate my trust in His wisdom and my commitment to living according to His standards. This obedience shapes my character and deepens my relationship with Him.

Additionally, pleasing God involves a commitment to righteousness and integrity. I am called to live a life that reflects His holiness, avoiding behaviors and attitudes that contradict His teachings. This pursuit of righteousness is not about achieving perfection but about striving to align more closely with His character. It means making choices that honor Him and reflect His moral and ethical standards.

Equally important is the call to love others as God loves me. In John 15:12, Jesus commands us to "love one another as I have loved you." This love is the cornerstone of living a life that pleases God. It involves showing kindness, compassion, and forgiveness, even when it is difficult. By loving others selflessly, I reflect His love and contribute to His work in the world.

Living to please God also means being a good steward of the gifts and resources He has entrusted to me. Whether it is my time, talents, or finances, I am called to use them in ways that advance His Kingdom and serve others. This stewardship reflects a heart that values His blessings and desires to honor Him through responsible and generous living.

In practical terms, this means making daily decisions with a focus on His will. It involves seeking His guidance through prayer and meditation, and making choices that align with His teachings. Each decision, no matter how small, can be an opportunity to honor Him and reflect His values. By consistently choosing to follow His guidance, I create a life that is characterized by His peace and purpose.

Ultimately, living to please God is about cultivating a relationship with Him that permeates every aspect of my life. It is a journey of growing in faith, understanding, and love. As I seek to honor Him in all I do, I find a deep sense of fulfillment and joy that comes from knowing that my life aligns with His will and contributes to His greater purpose.

Living a life that pleases God is a profound and transformative journey. It involves aligning my actions, thoughts, and desires with His will, walking in obedience, reflecting His love, and being a good steward of His gifts. By focusing on these aspects, I strive to honor Him and contribute to His work in the world. This pursuit of a life that pleases God brings a deep sense of purpose and fulfillment, rooted in a relationship with Him that guides and sustains me in every aspect of my life.

In my walk with God, the truth that "With God, all things are possible" (Matthew 19:26) resonates deeply within me, offering both comfort and challenge. This profound declaration reassures me that no matter how insurmountable the obstacles or daunting the challenges, God's power transcends every limitation. When Jesus spoke these words to His disciples, He was emphasizing that human limitations are not a barrier to God's limitless potential. This understanding has become a cornerstone of my faith, guiding me to trust in His omnipotence and embrace the boundless possibilities that His presence brings into my life.

Every challenge I face is an opportunity to experience God's power at work. Whether I am navigating personal struggles, seeking guidance for major decisions, or grappling with uncertainties about the future, I am reminded that nothing is beyond God's ability to transform. This belief inspires me to approach each situation with faith, knowing that my strength and perseverance are not solely dependent on my own capabilities but on the infinite resources and wisdom that God provides. By placing my trust in Him, I am inviting His miraculous power into every aspect of my life.

Furthermore, understanding that "With God, all things are possible" encourages me to dream bigger and hope more profoundly. It reshapes my perspective from one of limitation to one of possibility, inviting me to step beyond my comfort zones and embrace the extraordinary plans God has for me. This realization is both empowering and humbling, as it reminds me that while I may face limitations as a human being, God's ability to accomplish His will is not constrained by any earthly barriers. It motivates me to pursue my goals with confidence and to trust in His guidance as I seek to fulfill the purpose He has set for me.

Central to realizing the possibilities that God offers is adhering to His instructions. John 14:18 reassures me of His commitment to not leave me as an orphan but to come to me, providing the guidance and support I need. This verse underscores the importance of staying connected to Him and seeking His direction in all aspects of my life. When I am faced with decisions or challenges, I am reminded to turn to God for instruction, trusting that His guidance is always in alignment with His perfect will for my life.

Following God's instructions involves more than just reading the Scriptures; it requires an active engagement with His Word and an openness to His leading through the Holy Spirit. It is about cultivating a relationship with God that allows me to hear His voice clearly and respond with obedience. This relationship is built through prayer, meditation, and a continuous study of His Word, which provides me with the clarity and wisdom needed to navigate life's complexities.

Obeying God's instructions is not always easy, but it is essential for experiencing the fullness of His promises. His guidance often calls me to step out in faith, to make choices that align with His will, and to trust in His timing. This obedience is a testament to my faith and trust in His plan, demonstrating a willingness to submit my own desires and plans to His greater purpose. As I follow His instructions, I align myself with His will, opening the door to His transformative power and the fulfillment of His promises in my life.

Moreover, living according to God's instructions involves a commitment to integrity and authenticity. It requires me to align my actions with His teachings, ensuring that my life reflects the values and principles He has outlined. This alignment is not just about outward compliance but about a heart transformation that seeks to honor Him in all things. By living in accordance with His Word, I demonstrate my commitment to His will and invite His blessings and guidance into my life.

In practical terms, following God's instructions means seeking His guidance in every decision I make, whether it concerns my career, relationships, or personal growth. It involves discerning His will through prayer, seeking counsel from wise and godly individuals, and aligning my choices with His teachings. This proactive approach to following His guidance ensures that I remain on the path He has set for me, experiencing the peace and assurance that comes from walking in His will.

In conclusion, the truth that "With God, all things are possible" is a powerful reminder of His limitless power and the boundless possibilities He offers. It inspires me to trust in His omnipotence, embrace the opportunities He provides, and pursue my goals with faith and confidence. Coupled with this belief is the necessity of following God's instructions, which involves seeking His guidance, obeying His Word, and living in alignment with His will. By integrating these principles into my life, I position myself to experience the fullness of His promises and to walk in the path He has laid out for me. In this journey, I am continuously reminded that with God, indeed, all things are possible, and His guidance is the key to unlocking the extraordinary potential He has in store.

In the journey of singleness, it's crucial to embrace the profound truth that with God, all things are possible. This realization has become a cornerstone of my faith and daily living, guiding me to approach every challenge and opportunity with unwavering confidence in God's limitless power. As a single person, I understand that this phase of life can bring its own set of struggles and uncertainties, but I am here to affirm that you don't have to face these struggles alone. Instead, you can live victoriously and fully embrace the truth that God's promises are not limited by our circumstances.

The idea that "with God, all things are possible" is not just a comforting thought but a dynamic reality that has the power to transform our lives. When we recognize that God's power is boundless and that He is actively involved in our lives, we can approach each day with a sense of hope and expectation. This truth has been a guiding force in my own life, particularly during times when I felt overwhelmed or unsure about the future. Understanding that God's capabilities surpass all earthly limitations empowers me to face challenges with faith rather than fear.

One of the most profound aspects of this truth is the assurance that no matter what I am going through—whether it's facing personal struggles, navigating career challenges, or dealing with relational issues—I am not alone. God's omnipotence means that He is more than capable of handling any situation that arises. This has been particularly comforting during times of uncertainty or difficulty, reminding me that even when I feel inadequate or overwhelmed, God's strength and ability are more than sufficient. By leaning into His power, I am able to overcome obstacles that might otherwise seem insurmountable.

Living victoriously as a single person involves understanding that our value and worth are not defined by our relationship status but by our identity in Christ. This has been a crucial realization for me, as it has allowed me to embrace my singleness with confidence and purpose. Knowing that I am beloved and valued by God, regardless of my marital status, enables me to live each day with a sense of purpose and fulfillment. My worth is not contingent on whether or not I am married but on the unchanging truth that I am a child of God, created in His image and loved beyond measure.

The concept of living victoriously also means recognizing that God has a unique plan and purpose for each of us, irrespective of our current circumstances. For me, this has involved embracing opportunities for personal growth, pursuing passions and interests, and engaging in activities that align with God's calling on my life. By focusing on living out my purpose and contributing positively to those around me, I am able to find joy and satisfaction in my singleness. This perspective shift helps me to see my current state not as a limitation but as a season filled with potential and possibilities.

Moreover, understanding that "with God, all things are possible" encourages me to approach life with a mindset of expectancy. It reminds me that God is always at work, even when I cannot see immediate results. This mindset fosters resilience and hope, allowing me to persevere through challenging times with the assurance that God is guiding and supporting me. By maintaining a positive outlook and trusting in His plans, I am better equipped to navigate the ups and downs of life with grace and optimism.

In practical terms, living victoriously means actively engaging in practices that strengthen my faith and relationship with God. This includes regular prayer, studying Scripture, and seeking guidance through meditation and reflection. These practices are not just routine activities but essential elements of nurturing a deeper connection with God. They provide me with spiritual nourishment and insight, helping me to stay grounded and focused on His promises. By prioritizing these practices, I am able to cultivate a vibrant faith that sustains me through every season of life.

Another vital aspect of living victoriously is embracing the support and community available to me. Engaging with a faith community and building meaningful relationships with others who share my values provides a source of encouragement and accountability. This sense of belonging helps me to stay connected to others who can offer support and share in my journey. By participating in community activities, sharing experiences, and providing support to others, I contribute to a network of mutual encouragement and growth.

The journey of singleness also presents opportunities for self-discovery and personal development. It is a time to explore and cultivate my talents, interests, and passions. By investing in personal growth and pursuing goals that align with my values and aspirations, I am able to make the most of this season. This proactive approach allows me to build a fulfilling and purposeful life, preparing me for the future and equipping me to contribute positively to the world around me.

In reflecting on my own experiences, I recognize that there have been moments of doubt and struggle. However, it is in these moments that the truth of God's promise that "with God, all things are possible" becomes even more evident. Each challenge has been an opportunity to witness His faithfulness and experience His provision. By leaning into His strength and trusting in His plans, I am able to overcome difficulties and find renewed hope and confidence.

Ultimately, living victoriously as a single person involves embracing the truth that God's power and possibilities extend to every aspect of our lives. It means recognizing that our current circumstances do not define our future but rather serve as a stage for experiencing God's work and transformation. By trusting in His promises, pursuing personal growth, engaging with community, and maintaining a sense of hope and expectancy, we can navigate singleness with grace and purpose.

The belief that "with God, all things are possible" is a powerful truth that can transform our approach to singleness and life's challenges. It offers reassurance and encouragement, reminding us that we are not limited by our circumstances but empowered by God's limitless power. By embracing this truth, living with purpose, and following His guidance, we can experience victory and fulfillment in every season of life. As I continue to walk this journey, I am continually reminded that with God, indeed, all things are possible, and His promises are a source of strength and hope for every aspect of my life.

In my spiritual journey, I've come to deeply appreciate the vital importance of receiving my instructions directly from God. This principle has become a cornerstone of my faith and practice, guiding me through every decision and challenge I face. The process of seeking and following divine instructions is not just a routine but a profound relationship that shapes my path and helps me align with God's will.

To get instructions from God involves a heartfelt commitment to prayer, reflection, and attentiveness. I've learned that God's guidance often comes in subtle ways—through Scripture, the inner voice of the Holy Spirit, or through circumstances and people that He places in my life. It requires a posture of openness and receptivity, where I am willing to listen and discern His will amidst the noise and distractions of everyday life. This practice of seeking God's instructions ensures that I am moving in the direction that He has planned for me, rather than relying solely on my own understanding or the influence of external forces.

Trusting in God's instructions has been essential in my journey to please Him. It's about aligning my actions and decisions with His divine will, even when it might not align with my immediate desires or plans. This trust is built on a foundation of faith, acknowledging that God's plans for me are always for my good, even when the path seems unclear or challenging. By adhering to His guidance, I find a deeper sense of purpose and fulfillment, knowing that I am walking in step with His divine plan.

The contrast between following God's instructions and being a slave to Satan is stark and profound. While I strive to live in accordance with God's will, I recognize that deviating from this path opens the door to influences that can lead me away from Him. Being a slave to Satan, in this context, means surrendering to forces that seek to undermine God's work in my life—whether through temptation, deceit, or distraction. It's a reminder of the spiritual battle that we face and the need for vigilance and commitment to God's instructions.

Remaining true to God's guidance involves constant vigilance and discipline. It means being alert to the subtle ways in which negative influences might seek to sway me from the path of righteousness. This awareness helps me to stay focused on God's word and His promises, ensuring that I am not easily swayed by worldly temptations or doubts. It's a daily choice to align my will with His, seeking His instructions and trusting that they lead to a life that is fulfilling and pleasing to Him.

In practical terms, getting instructions from God also involves engaging with His word regularly. Scripture provides a solid foundation for understanding His will and offers practical guidance for daily living. By immersing myself in the Bible, I gain insight into His character, His promises, and His expectations. This engagement with His word helps me to discern His voice more clearly and to follow His guidance with confidence.

Additionally, the role of prayer in this process cannot be overstated. Through prayer, I communicate with God, seeking His direction and clarity. It is a time to express my desires, fears, and needs, and to listen for His response. This dialogue with God strengthens my relationship with Him and ensures that I am attuned to His instructions. Prayer is not just a ritual but a vital part of my spiritual life that fosters a deeper connection with the divine.

As I reflect on the importance of following God's instructions, I am reminded of the profound impact that this practice has on my life. It shapes my decisions, influences my relationships, and guides my actions. By staying committed to His guidance, I experience a sense of peace and assurance, knowing that I am walking in alignment with His will. This alignment brings a deep sense of fulfillment and purpose, as I trust that my life is being directed by a loving and all-knowing God.

In contrast, the alternative of being a slave to Satan represents a path of spiritual confusion and distress. It's a path that leads away from God's truth and into a realm of deception and bondage. Recognizing this reality helps me to stay vigilant and committed to seeking God's instructions. It reinforces my resolve to live according to His will and to reject any influences that seek to pull me away from His path.

The journey of receiving and following instructions from God is a profound and transformative experience. It requires dedication, prayer, and a willingness to align my life with His will. By staying true to His guidance, I can navigate life's challenges with confidence, knowing that I am walking in step with a divine plan that is both purposeful and fulfilling. This commitment to God's instructions not only shapes my personal journey but also reflects a deep trust in His sovereignty and love. As I continue on this path, I am continually reminded of the importance of seeking His guidance and staying true to His will, ensuring that I remain aligned with His purpose and live a life that is pleasing to Him.

As a single woman, one of the most profound lessons I've learned is the necessity of avoiding double-mindedness in my spiritual journey. The essence of being purposeful in my singleness is deeply intertwined with the clarity and focus of my thoughts and intentions. Matthew 6:22 resonates deeply with me: "The eye is the lamp of the body. If your eyes are healthy, your whole body will be full of light." This scripture emphasizes the importance of having a clear and single vision, which is crucial for living a life that is both purposeful and aligned with God's will.

When I reflect on this verse, I understand it as an encouragement to maintain a clear and unwavering focus in my spiritual life. Double-mindedness, as described in James 1:8, suggests a lack of stability and consistency in our faith and actions. For me, it means that I cannot afford to be swayed by conflicting desires, doubts, or distractions. Instead, I must cultivate a single-minded devotion to God, ensuring that my heart and mind are fully aligned with His will.

Being purposeful in my singleness requires a deep and abiding clarity of vision. It's about setting my sights firmly on the goals that God has placed before me and avoiding the pitfalls of distraction and indecision. Just as a healthy eye brings light to the body, a focused and undivided heart brings light and purpose to my life. This clarity allows me to make decisions that reflect my commitment to God's purpose, rather than being torn between conflicting desires or uncertainties.

In practical terms, avoiding double-mindedness involves being intentional about my choices and priorities. I find it essential to regularly assess my goals and ensure that they are aligned with God's plans for me. This means engaging in regular prayer, seeking His guidance, and reflecting on His word to maintain a clear understanding of His will. By doing so, I keep my focus sharp and my path illuminated, ensuring that I am not swayed by external pressures or internal conflicts.

Moreover, maintaining a single vision involves setting boundaries and making choices that reflect my commitment to God. It's about being deliberate in how I spend my time, energy, and resources, ensuring that these are directed toward goals that align with His purpose. This intentional living helps me to stay on course and avoid the pitfalls of distraction and wavering.

Another important aspect of avoiding double-mindedness is dealing with doubt and uncertainty. There are moments when I may question my path or feel uncertain about the future. During these times, it is crucial for me to return to God's word and seek reassurance and clarity. By anchoring myself in His promises and trusting in His guidance, I am able to overcome doubt and maintain a steadfast focus on His purpose for my life.

As a single woman, I also recognize the importance of surrounding myself with supportive and like-minded individuals who encourage me in my journey. Engaging with a community of faith provides me with accountability and support, helping me to stay focused on my goals and avoid the pitfalls of double-mindedness. This fellowship serves as a reminder of God's promises and helps me to stay grounded in His truth.

In my pursuit of purpose, I also find that it is essential to address and manage any competing desires or distractions that may arise. This might involve making difficult choices or letting go of things that do not align with my spiritual goals. By being honest with myself and seeking God's guidance, I am able to make decisions that keep me focused and aligned with His will.

Ultimately, being a purposeful single woman involves a commitment to living with intention and clarity. It means avoiding the confusion and instability that comes from double-mindedness and instead cultivating a clear and singular vision for my life. By doing so,

I am able to live in a way that is both fulfilling and aligned with God's purpose, ensuring that my actions and decisions reflect my dedication to His will.

Matthew 6:22 serves as a powerful reminder of the importance of having a clear and focused vision in my spiritual journey. By avoiding double-mindedness and maintaining a single-hearted devotion to God, I can navigate my path with confidence and purpose. This clarity allows me to make decisions that reflect His will and to live a life that is both purposeful and fulfilling. As I continue to seek His guidance and align my actions with His purpose, I am continually reminded of the significance of living with intention and maintaining a clear and unwavering focus on His plans for my life.

As a single person, one of the most crucial aspects of my spiritual journey is the need to avoid double-mindedness. It's something I've come to understand deeply, recognizing how essential it is for maintaining clarity and purpose in my life. To be double-minded is to waver between conflicting desires or beliefs, leading to instability and confusion. For me, it means that I must strive for a singular focus and unwavering commitment to God's will, avoiding the pitfalls of indecision and distraction that can so easily derail my path.

Being single offers a unique opportunity to cultivate a deep and consistent relationship with God, and this period of my life can be a time of profound growth and purpose. However, if I allow myself to be double-minded, I risk undermining the potential of this season. I've learned that double-mindedness is not merely a matter of occasional doubt but can become a persistent state of uncertainty that affects every area of my life. When my heart and mind are not fully aligned with God's will, it becomes difficult to make decisions, set priorities, and pursue goals with confidence.

To combat double-mindedness, I first need to establish a strong foundation in my faith. This means immersing myself in God's word, seeking His guidance through prayer, and surrounding myself with supportive and like-minded individuals who encourage my spiritual growth. By anchoring myself in these practices, I am able to maintain a clear sense of direction and purpose, ensuring that my decisions and actions reflect my commitment to His will.

Another key aspect of avoiding double-mindedness is making intentional choices that align with my spiritual goals. This involves evaluating my priorities and ensuring that they are in harmony with God's plans for my life. I've found that when I make decisions based on what I believe God is calling me to do, rather than being swayed by external pressures or conflicting desires, I am more likely to experience a sense of fulfillment and clarity. It's about living with intention and purpose, rather than being tossed about by the whims of circumstance or the opinions of others.

Additionally, addressing and managing competing desires is crucial in my journey to avoid double-mindedness. There are times when I may feel torn between different aspirations or interests, and it can be challenging to discern which path aligns best with God's will. During these moments, I rely on prayer and reflection to seek His guidance and gain clarity. By focusing on what truly matters and seeking His direction, I am able to make decisions that reflect my commitment to His purpose and avoid the confusion that comes from being double-minded.

Maintaining a clear vision also involves setting boundaries and being mindful of how I spend my time and energy. As a single person, I have the opportunity to invest in personal growth, ministry, and other areas that align with God's purpose for me. By being deliberate in how I use my resources and making choices that reflect my values and goals, I am able to stay focused and avoid the distractions that can lead to double-mindedness.

Furthermore, I've learned the importance of cultivating a mindset of trust and reliance on God's timing and plans. It's easy to become anxious or uncertain when things don't go as expected or when I face challenges. However, by placing my trust in His promises and recognizing that He is in control, I can maintain a sense of peace and stability. Trusting in His timing helps me to avoid the instability that comes from being double-minded and allows me to move forward with confidence.

In practical terms, avoiding double-mindedness also means being honest with myself about my motivations and desires. I've found that self-reflection and accountability are essential for identifying areas where I might be wavering or conflicted. By addressing these issues openly and seeking support from trusted friends or mentors, I can gain insight and make more informed decisions that align with God's will.

Ultimately, avoiding double-mindedness is about living with a sense of purpose and commitment to God's plans. It's about ensuring that my thoughts, actions, and decisions reflect my dedication to His will and avoiding the confusion and instability that come from conflicting desires. By focusing on His guidance, setting intentional goals, and trusting in His timing, I can navigate my journey as a single person with clarity and confidence.

Avoiding double-mindedness is a crucial aspect of living a purposeful and fulfilling life as a single person. By maintaining a clear vision, making intentional choices, and trusting in God's guidance, I can navigate my path with stability and purpose. This period of singleness offers a unique opportunity to grow in my faith and align my life with God's will, and by addressing the challenges of double-mindedness, I can fully embrace the potential of this season and move forward with confidence and clarity.

In Luke 11:3, Jesus instructs us to pray, "Give us day by day our daily bread." This scripture resonates deeply with me, as it encapsulates the essence of daily dependence on God. Each day, I am reminded that my needs, both physical and spiritual, are continually met by God's provision. This verse is a call to trust in God's daily sustenance. As I navigate the complexities of life, this daily prayer reminds me to acknowledge that my sustenance comes from God alone. It's not just about physical food but also the spiritual nourishment I need to thrive. By asking for daily bread, I am expressing my reliance on God's provision and acknowledging that He is the source of all that I need. This practice of daily dependence helps me cultivate a deeper relationship with God, recognizing that He is the provider of every good gift. Each day, as I pray for my daily bread, I am reminded to focus on today, trusting that God will take care of my needs for today and every day.

John 3:16 – "For God so loved the world that He gave His only begotten Son, that whoever believes in Him should not perish but have everlasting life."

John 3:16 is perhaps one of the most profound and comforting verses in the Bible. The depth of God's love for humanity is displayed in this verse, where it is declared that God loved the world so much that He gave His only Son, Jesus Christ, for our salvation. This act of sacrificial love is the foundation of my faith. It assures me that no matter how flawed I may feel or how far I have strayed, God's love is unwavering and unconditional. Jesus's sacrifice on the cross is the ultimate expression of divine love and grace. Believing in Him grants me the promise of eternal life, a gift that I could never earn on my own. This verse continually reminds me of the incredible sacrifice made for my sake and the boundless love that God has for me and for all humanity. It calls me to respond to this love with gratitude and a life that reflects His teachings and example. Understanding this verse helps me grasp the magnitude of God's grace and motivates me to live in a way that honors this profound gift.

2 Corinthians 4:4 – "In whom the god of this world hath blinded the minds of them which believe not, lest the light of the glorious gospel of Christ, who is the image of God, should shine unto them."

2 Corinthians 4:4 speaks to the spiritual blindness that affects those who do not believe in Christ. This verse reveals a crucial aspect of the spiritual battle that I face. The "god of this world" refers to Satan, who blinds the minds of unbelievers to keep them from seeing the light of the gospel. This blindness is not a physical sight but a spiritual darkness that prevents people from recognizing the truth and beauty of Christ's message. As I reflect on this scripture, I am reminded of the importance of prayer and intercession for those who have not yet experienced the light of the gospel. It also serves as a reminder of my own need for continual spiritual awareness and vigilance.

Understanding this verse encourages me to share the gospel with compassion and persistence, knowing that it is only through the work of the Holy Spirit that hearts and minds can be opened to the truth. This verse underscores the significance of divine intervention in the process of salvation and the role I play in spreading the light of Christ to others.

Expounding on these scriptures as a cohesive reflection:

As I meditate on Luke 11:3, John 3:16, and 2 Corinthians 4:4, I am drawn into a deeper understanding of my faith and my relationship with God. These verses collectively illustrate the essence of divine provision, sacrificial love, and the spiritual struggle against blindness.

Luke 11:3 reminds me daily of my dependence on God. Each day, as I ask for my "daily bread," I acknowledge God as the provider of all that I need. This request goes beyond physical sustenance; it encompasses the spiritual nourishment required to live a faithful and purposeful life. It is an invitation to trust in God's daily provision, acknowledging that His care is ongoing and sufficient for each moment.

John 3:16 reinforces the incredible love that God has for me and the entire world. The fact that God gave His only Son for my salvation is a profound expression of divine love and grace. This sacrificial act is the cornerstone of my faith and the source of my hope for eternal life. It is a reminder that no matter the struggles or imperfections I face, God's love remains steadfast and unchanging. This verse calls me to live in response to this love, embodying the grace and forgiveness that Jesus has shown me.

2 Corinthians 4:4 highlights the spiritual reality of blindness that affects those who do not yet believe in Christ. This verse illuminates the challenge of sharing the gospel and the importance of divine intervention in opening hearts and minds to the truth. It reminds me of the spiritual warfare that occurs and the need for prayer and reliance on the Holy Spirit's power. My role in this battle is to be a beacon of light,

sharing the gospel with sincerity and compassion, while recognizing that only God can remove the blindness and bring others into the light of His truth.

Together, these scriptures guide me in understanding the fullness of God's provision, the depth of His love, and the spiritual dynamics at play in the mission of spreading the gospel. They shape my daily walk, encouraging me to rely on God's daily provision, to live in response to His sacrificial love, and to engage actively in sharing the light of Christ with those who are spiritually blinded. In this way, I strive to align my life with these profound truths, living out my faith with purpose and dedication.

Luke 11:3 – "Give us day by day our daily bread."

When I reflect on Luke 11:3, where Jesus instructs us to pray for our daily bread, I'm reminded of the profound simplicity and depth of this request. Every day, as I ask God for my daily bread, I'm acknowledging my absolute reliance on Him for both my physical needs and my spiritual nourishment. This daily petition is not just about asking for food; it's about recognizing that each day is a gift from God and that His provision is essential for my well-being. The act of asking for daily bread is a practice of faith, a moment-by-moment trust in God's goodness and His promises. It's a declaration that my life is sustained by His grace and that I cannot rely on my strength or resources alone. This daily dependence on God helps me stay grounded and humble, understanding that my sustenance, my strength, and my very life come from Him. By seeking His provision daily, I remain connected to Him, acknowledging that He is the source of all my needs and that His faithfulness endures every day.

John 3:16 – "For God so loved the world that He gave His only begotten Son, that whoever believes in Him should not perish but have everlasting life."

John 3:16 is a cornerstone of my faith, representing the ultimate expression of God's love for humanity. When I ponder this verse, I am struck by the magnitude of God's sacrifice in giving His only Son, Jesus Christ, for my salvation. This verse encapsulates the gospel message: that through Jesus's sacrifice, I am offered the gift of eternal life, regardless of my past or present circumstances. It's a reminder that God's love is not limited or conditional; it's a boundless, all-encompassing love that reaches out to every person. This understanding of God's love inspires me to live a life of gratitude and purpose. It challenges me to reflect that same love in my interactions with others, to be a vessel of His grace and truth. This verse also reassures me that my worth is not determined by my achievements or failures but by the love and sacrifice of Jesus. As I embrace this truth, I am motivated to share this message of hope and redemption with others, knowing that it is through belief in Jesus that they, too, can experience eternal life.

2 Corinthians 4:4 – "In whom the god of this world hath blinded the minds of them which believe not, lest the light of the glorious gospel of Christ, who is the image of God, should shine unto them."

In 2 Corinthians 4:4, Paul addresses the spiritual blindness that prevents many from recognizing the truth of the gospel. This verse brings to light the reality that there are spiritual forces at work, specifically the "god of this world," who blinds the minds of those who do not believe. This blindness is a significant barrier to understanding and accepting the gospel message. As I reflect on this scripture, I'm reminded of the spiritual battle that underlies evangelism and the importance of prayer in overcoming this blindness. It encourages me to remain vigilant and compassionate in my efforts to share the gospel, recognizing that it's not merely a matter of presenting facts but a profound spiritual intervention. This verse also serves as a reminder of the power of the gospel to shine through even the darkest of hearts and minds. It challenges me to trust in the effectiveness of God's word and to rely on the Holy Spirit's work in breaking through spiritual barriers.

By understanding this dynamic, I am better equipped to engage in meaningful dialogue about faith and to pray fervently for those who have not yet experienced the light of Christ.

Bringing these reflections together:

In my journey of faith, Luke 11:3, John 3:16, and 2 Corinthians 4:4 offer profound insights into how I am to live and interact with the world. Luke 11:3 teaches me daily dependence on God's provision, reminding me to trust Him for my needs and to remain connected to His grace each day. John 3:16 reveals the depth of God's love through Jesus's sacrifice, encouraging me to live a life that reflects this love and to share the message of eternal life with others. 2 Corinthians 4:4 highlights the spiritual blindness that can obscure the truth of the gospel, urging me to engage in prayer and compassion as I share the light of Christ.

These scriptures collectively shape my understanding of God's role in my life and in the world. They guide me in how to approach my daily needs, how to respond to God's love, and how to overcome the challenges of spiritual blindness. Each verse provides a different but complementary perspective on living a faithful and purposeful life, helping me navigate my journey with a deeper awareness of God's provision, love, and the spiritual dynamics at play.

By integrating these insights into my daily walk, I am equipped to live in a way that honors God, reflects His love, and engages meaningfully with the world around me. These scriptures remind me that, through God's grace and the power of His word, I can face daily challenges, live out His love, and be an instrument in bringing others into the light of the gospel.

Praying For A Spouse

In the depths of my heart, I harbor a profound desire to be married again, and I turn to God with this longing, asking Him to send me a husband who is not just any man but one who is ordained and sent by Him. This prayer is not a mere wish or a fleeting thought but a deeply held aspiration rooted in faith and trust in God's divine plan for my life. I am committed to seeking a relationship that aligns with His purpose and reflects His grace and love, and I am open to the journey He has in store for me.

As I navigate this season of my life, I find solace in the knowledge that God's plans are always perfect and His timing impeccable. I have learned through my experiences that what may seem like a delay or uncertainty is often a period of preparation and growth. My desire for marriage is not just about finding companionship but about entering into a union that is blessed by God and designed to fulfill His purposes. I am seeking a partner who will join me in serving the Lord, who will be my spiritual equal, and who will share in the mission of advancing His Kingdom.

In my prayers, I ask God to reveal to me the qualities and characteristics that He desires in a spouse for me. I pray for wisdom to recognize the man who is truly sent by Him, someone whose heart is aligned with His will and whose life is a reflection of His love and teachings. I seek a partner who embodies integrity, kindness, humility, and a deep commitment to faith, one who will support me in my journey of spiritual growth and in living out God's purpose for our lives together.

I am also mindful of the importance of being prepared myself. I understand that in order to receive a partner who is aligned with God's plan, I must be in a place of readiness and openness. This means continually seeking God's guidance, growing in my own faith, and being open to His will in all aspects of my life. I am committed to living a life that is pleasing to Him, focusing on spiritual growth, and being a vessel of His love and grace.

The desire to be married again is accompanied by a profound trust in God's timing. I know that He is working behind the scenes, preparing both me and the person He has chosen for me. My role is to remain patient, to continue seeking Him, and to trust that He is orchestrating every detail of my journey. I believe that God's timing is perfect, and that He will bring the right person into my life at the right moment.

As I pray for this God-ordained spouse, I am also mindful of the need to be proactive in seeking His guidance and direction. This includes being open to the ways in which He might lead me, whether through personal growth, community involvement, or even through the people He places in my path. I am committed to being attentive to His voice and responsive to His leading, knowing that He will guide me toward the man who is meant to be my partner.

My desire for a husband who is sent by God is also a desire for a relationship that is grounded in mutual respect, love, and faith. I envision a partnership where both of us are committed to growing together in our relationship with God, where we support and encourage each other in our spiritual journeys, and where our marriage becomes a testament to His love and grace. I long for a relationship that not only fulfills our personal desires but also serves as a witness to the power of God's love and His ability to bring people together according to His perfect plan.

My desire to be married again is a heartfelt prayer for a God-ordained spouse who is sent by Him. I am committed to seeking His will, preparing myself for the right relationship, and trusting in His perfect timing. I believe that God has a plan for my life that includes a partner who will complement and support me in fulfilling His purposes. As I continue to pray and seek His guidance, I hold fast to the promise that with God, all things are possible, and that He will bring into my life the man who is meant to be my husband. Through faith, patience, and trust in His divine plan, I am confident that God will answer this prayer and fulfill the deepest desires of my heart.

In my quest for companionship and marriage, I find myself yearning for more than just any partner. I am seeking someone who is not only a loving and supportive spouse but also a person who is deeply filled with the Holy Spirit and wholly committed to a mission for the Lord. This journey is not simply about finding someone to share my life with; it is about finding a partner who will walk beside me in our shared devotion to God, someone whose life is a testament to His power and purpose.

The desire for a Spirit-filled partner stems from a profound understanding of the importance of spiritual unity in a relationship. A marriage grounded in shared faith and mutual devotion to God is one where both individuals can grow together in their spiritual journey, supporting and encouraging each other in their walk with the Lord. This vision of marriage goes beyond mere compatibility and enters into a realm where both partners are committed to living out their faith actively and vibrantly.

To me, a Spirit-filled partner is someone who not only believes in God but experiences His presence and guidance in their daily life. Such a person is marked by the fruits of the Spirit: love, joy, peace, patience, kindness, goodness, faithfulness, gentleness, and self-control. These qualities are not just aspirations but are evident in their interactions, decisions, and overall way of life. I envision a relationship where these attributes are not only present but are actively cultivated and nurtured.

In seeking a partner who is on a mission for the Lord, I am looking for someone who is dedicated to advancing God's Kingdom, who is passionate about serving others, and who is actively involved in ministry or outreach. This mission-driven mindset reflects a commitment to living a life of purpose and impact, aligning with my own calling to serve and honor God in all aspects of my life. Together, we would work towards shared goals that honor God and contribute to the betterment of those around us, finding fulfillment in our joint efforts to make a difference.

The journey to finding such a partner is one of deep prayer and discernment. I am constantly seeking God's guidance, asking Him to reveal the qualities and characteristics that He desires in a spouse for me. My prayer is that He would lead me to someone whose heart is aligned with His will, whose mission is clear, and whose life is a reflection of His love and grace. I trust that God knows my heart's desires and will bring into my life the person who is meant to be my partner in this spiritual journey.

Moreover, I am committed to being the kind of partner that I seek. This involves continually growing in my own faith, deepening my relationship with God, and actively participating in His mission. I recognize that in order to attract a Spirit-filled and mission-driven spouse, I must embody these qualities myself. My goal is to be a person who reflects the love and light of Christ in all that I do, preparing myself to enter into a relationship that is grounded in shared faith and purpose.

As I navigate this path, I am also aware of the importance of being open to God's timing and leading. Finding a partner who meets these spiritual criteria may not happen according to my own timetable, but I trust in God's perfect timing and plan. I am patient and expectant, knowing that He is working behind the scenes to bring about the right circumstances and the right person into my life.

In the meantime, I remain focused on my own spiritual growth and the mission that God has set before me. I engage in activities and ministries that align with my calling, seeking to make a positive impact in the lives of others and to further His Kingdom. I am confident that as I continue to seek God and live out my faith, He will bring into my life the partner who will complement and support me in this journey.

My desire is to find a partner who is not just anyone but someone who is filled with the Holy Spirit and dedicated to a mission for the Lord. I am seeking a relationship where both individuals are committed to spiritual growth, mutual support, and active participation in God's work. Through prayer, discernment, and faithfulness, I trust that God will lead me to the right person, and together we will walk in His purpose, making a meaningful impact in our lives and in the world around us.

Epilogue:

The Purpose of Being Single: Embracing God's Plan and Walking in His Word

As we conclude this journey through the purpose and potential of singleness, I want to leave you with a message of hope, encouragement, and affirmation. Embracing your singleness is not merely about enduring a season of waiting or feeling incomplete. It is about recognizing and celebrating the unique opportunities that come with this stage of life, and aligning yourself with God's divine plan.

Singleness, as we've explored, is a time of profound growth and transformation. It is an invitation to delve deeply into your relationship with God, to discover and cultivate your purpose, and to prepare yourself for the future that He has in store. This period allows for a focus on personal development, spiritual enrichment, and service to others without the immediate responsibilities that come with marriage or family life. It is an opportunity to build a strong foundation of faith and character, to understand God's will more fully, and to walk in His ways with clarity and purpose.

Throughout this book, we have examined how to navigate singleness with grace and conviction. We have discussed the importance of aligning our lives with God's Word, seeking His guidance, and embracing the role He has called us to. Whether it is through prayer, service, or personal growth, each step taken in faith contributes to the fulfillment of His promises. The journey of being single can be a powerful and rewarding experience if approached with a heart willing to listen and a spirit eager to obey.

I encourage you to remember that your worth is not defined by your marital status but by your identity in Christ. God sees your heart, your struggles, and your desires, and He values you beyond measure. In moments of uncertainty or longing, lean into His promises, knowing that He is faithful to guide you and provide for you. Trust that His plans for you are good and that He is working all things together for your good.

Embrace this time as a precious gift, an opportunity to grow closer to God and to become the person He has designed you to be. Engage in His Word, seek His wisdom, and allow Him to shape your life in ways that bring glory to Him and blessings to those around you. The journey of singleness is not one of solitude or inadequacy but one of purpose and potential.

As you move forward, carry with you the assurance that God's plan for your life is unfolding according to His perfect timing. Be encouraged that you are not alone in this journey and that you have the support of a loving God who is always with you. Continue to walk in faith, seek His guidance, and live out His Word with conviction and joy.

Thank you for joining me on this exploration of the purpose of being single. May you find peace, fulfillment, and a deep sense of purpose as you embrace your singleness and walk steadfastly in God's plan for your life.

With blessings and encouragement,
Lillian Carlene Porter

Meet the Author

Lillian Carlene Porter is a devoted woman of faith whose life story is both inspiring and impactful. She accepted Christ as her personal Savior at the tender age of 12 and, by the age of 16, was already dedicated to serving Him wholeheartedly. Her parents, Ruth and Lyman Porter, provided a strong foundation of support and love throughout her formative years. In addition, her faithful praying partner, Versaline Williams, played a vital role in her spiritual journey, offering prayers that brought comfort and guidance.

From a young age, Lillian exhibited a nurturing spirit, taking on caregiving responsibilities even at the age of 10. Her early struggles with severe asthma taught her the profound power of prayer, as her mother's earnest prayers were a source of healing and strength. Lillian's passion for cooking and serving others has been a consistent theme throughout her life, reflecting her deep desire to help and uplift those around her.

Music has been another significant part of Lillian's life. She has spent years playing the piano and keyboard, finding both solace and joy in her musical pursuits. Her commitment to service extended beyond her immediate family; she has taken in and cared for several nieces, nephews, and even raised her great-niece, embodying a spirit of generosity and love.

A transformative period in Lillian's life came when she sought divine direction and clarity. Through studying the life of Moses and receiving spiritual insight, she gained a deeper understanding of her own path. This period of reflection led her to make significant life decisions, including navigating complex personal circumstances with prayerful consideration.

Throughout her journey, Lillian's unwavering love for the Lord has been the driving force behind her actions and decisions. Her life is a testament to faith, service, and continual personal growth, and she remains profoundly grateful for the guidance and strength that God has bestowed upon her.

Bibliography

The following scriptures were referenced throughout "The Purpose of Being Single: Embracing God's Plan and Walking in His Word" by Lillian Carlene Porter:

1. **2 Corinthians 1:20** - "For all the promises of God in Him are Yes, and in Him Amen, to the glory of God through us."

2. **1 Samuel 15:22** - "So Samuel said: 'Has the Lord as great delight in burnt offerings and sacrifices, As in obeying the voice of the Lord? Behold, to obey is better than sacrifice, And to heed than the fat of rams.'"

3. **Colossians 3:22** - "Bondservants, obey in all things your masters according to the flesh, not with eye-service, as men-pleasers, but in sincerity of heart, fearing God."

4. **Matthew 6:22** - "The lamp of the body is the eye. If therefore your eye is good, your whole body will be full of light."

5. **John 8:32** - "And you shall know the truth, and the truth shall make you free."

6. **Psalm 37:5** - "Commit your way to the Lord, Trust also in Him, And He shall bring it to pass."

7. **John 14:18** - "I will not leave you orphans; I will come to you."

8. **Luke 11:3** - "Give us day by day our daily bread."

9. **John 3:16** - "For God so loved the world that He gave His only begotten Son, that whoever believes in Him should not perish but have everlasting life."

10. **2 Corinthians 4:4** - "Whose minds the god of this age has blinded, who do not believe, lest the light of the gospel of the

glory of Christ, who is the image of God, should shine on them."

11. **Ephesians 6:5-9** - "Bondservants, be obedient to those who are your masters according to the flesh, with fear and trembling, in sincerity of heart, as to Christ; not with eye-service, as men-pleasers, but as bondservants of Christ, doing the will of God from the heart, with good will doing service, as to the Lord, and not to men, knowing that whatever good anyone does, he will receive the same from the Lord, whether he is a slave or free. And you, masters, do the same things to them, giving up threatening, knowing that your own Master also is in heaven, and there is no partiality with Him."

These scriptures form the basis for the discussions and reflections in the book, providing spiritual guidance and insights into embracing God's plan and living a purposeful life as a single individual.

www.ingramcontent.com/pod-product-compliance
Lightning Source LLC
Chambersburg PA
CBHW020601160726
47991CB00002B/818